Formation for ministry
within a learning church
Shaping the future

New patterns of training
for lay and ordained

Church House Publishing
Church House,

Great Smith Street,

London SW1P 3NZ

Tel: 020 7898 1594

Fax: 020 7898 1449

ISBN 0 7151 4090 6

Published 2006 for the Ministry Division of the Archbishops' Council
by Church House Publishing

Printed in England by The Cromwell Press, Trowbridge, Wiltshire

Contents

Part 3

Parameters of the Curriculum

and

Post-ordination phase of IME

Preface

Formation for Ministry within a Learning Church set out broad principles to guide our churches in the provision of education and formation in the coming decade. It has launched a far-reaching process of change, recently reaffirmed by the Church of England's General Synod at York in July 2005.. We are grateful for all the work that is going on in the establishing of appropriate structures in the regions. At the same time, task groups have been working up more detailed guidance on a range of educational and training issues. This work has been done through the task groups on Education for Discipleship, Reader/Preacher training, the ordination curriculum and the post-ordination phase of training. It is now presented together as, of course, one of our aims is for a much better integration of training for lay and ordained and before and after ordination. The Steering Group welcomes this work and the ecumenical spirit in which it has been done. It commends it to the dioceses, partner churches and training institutions as they take up the task of creating new patterns of training to serve our churches. We hope it will prove to be a valuable resource in the continuing work in this field.

✣ Chelmsford

Chair, Steering Group, Formation for Ministry within a Learning Church

September 2005

Part 1

Education for Discipleship

A report of the implementation task group

Section 1

Introduction

'Learning is a task and gift for the whole people of God.'
(Formation for Ministry within a Learning Church 4:1)

Background

The 'Education for Discipleship' (EFD) proposals grow out of the aspirations of the 2003 Report *Formation for Ministry within a Learning Church*, and the desire expressed for the whole Church to become a 'Learning Church'. To develop in this way the Church needs to involve many players and contributors. Recent years have seen a marked increase in the provision of enquirers', access and foundation courses in many individual congregations, dioceses and denominations. The following proposals for a structured 'Education for Discipleship' programme are offered so that, within the context of a Church engaged in the ongoing task of encouraging all Christians in their growing discipleship, opportunities are available to enable lay Christians to develop their learning further.

The 2003 report advocates further developing the scope for formal 'theological education benefiting lay and ordained alike'. It proposes building on basic courses offered to congregations and by dioceses, to extend further good practice in structured lay theological education. This already exists in some places, though current provision of such opportunities is not available everywhere. The report suggests developing academically accredited programmes that continue to extend and build on 'the great range of work currently done in dioceses and parishes, most of which is appropriately not accredited at HE level'. It suggests 'the focus would be on deepening the knowledge and understanding of the Christian faith in order to inform discipleship, ministry and mission' (5.22, 2003 report).

In addition, it is intended that some of these study opportunities could be valuable for potential candidates for ordination, and ensure that they are able to participate in some serious study prior to selection (5.23ff, 2003 report). The EFD programme has been asked to ensure that such opportunities are *'offered on a Church-wide basis'* so that any candidates can be encouraged to engage in them. The report does not impose an expectation that all ordinands will have completed identical work on a core curriculum prior to entering theological colleges or courses.

A third area where EFD programmes may play a part is as a partial contribution to some lay ministerial training (5.28, 2003 report). The modular pattern proposed for EFD will make it possible to identify some topics that could be used as part of Reader / Preacher training. Some could also helpfully complement training some dioceses and participating churches offer for a range of locally authorized lay ministries.

It is, however, important to recognize EFD demonstrates the churches' commitment to resourcing laity for their life in the world. Its prime focus is not church-based ministry.

The Education for Discipleship task group

The group was asked:

- to produce a national specification for structured 'Education for Discipleship' programmes;
- to give guidance to providers of training on the nature of programmes to be drawn up.

The group was also asked to liaise as necessary with other groups, especially the group looking at Reader training.

Membership:

- Miss Joanna Cox (Archbishops' Council Education Division – Chair)
- Mr Chris Peck (Peterborough Diocese: diocesan adult educator)
- The Revd David Jenkins (United Reformed Church)
- The Revd Canon Mark Sanders (St Edmundsbury & Ipswich: diocesan director of ordinands)
- The Revd Preb. David Sceats (North Thames Ministerial Training Course: college/course/scheme staff member)
- Dr Esther Shreeve (Methodist Church)
- Dr David Way (Archbishops' Council Ministry Division)

EFD and discipleship

The term 'discipleship' has been used in so many different ways that it now hardly has an agreed precise meaning. Its use is associated with a wide range of responses related to following, learning, obeying and growing – ideas deeply entrenched in common Christian consciousness. Sometimes its use in particular contexts also suggests assumptions, perspectives and values about church membership. As the word 'discipleship' is embodied in the 2003 report and is a key part of our brief, it seems helpful to clarify our understanding of it.

In this report, we use the term 'discipleship' to describe the whole life-response of Christians to Jesus Christ. Everything a Christian believes and does is potentially an aspect of discipleship: the goal of discipleship is to grow ever more Christ-like in every aspect of life.

The primary focus of discipleship is the service of God and his mission in the world. We recognize that many lay people see such service as their vocation and ministry, so that the term 'ministry' need not describe only those activities undertaken within frameworks established by the churches. However, in this document we have used the term 'discipleship' to help clarify the distinction between this lay service / ministry and that of publicly authorized ministry, with its key focus on the nurture, development and leadership of the Church and equipping others for service.

The tendency in our church culture is to see ordained ministry as a normative category for discipleship. This often leads to a church-orientated (and in our view, limited) approach to discipleship. The focus of much ordained ministry is the Church gathered together, while that of discipleship is the Church dispersed in the world. One primary goal is that disciples should be more Christ-like human beings. In so doing, they become more effective signs of God's kingdom and rule.

Misunderstandings of 'discipleship'

There are two current ways of describing discipleship that we do not adopt.

- In the context of education for various ministries publicly authorized by the Church, discipleship may be misunderstood as a preliminary foundational stage. 'Education for Discipleship' might then seem to refer to an access level on the pathway to 'ministry'.

  This is not what we mean by education for discipleship. We do not see public ministry as a higher or more sacred calling. All Christians are called to be disciples of Jesus. Authorized public ministry is one way in which Christian vocation to discipleship is worked out for some people. Education for Discipleship is undertaken to help people be better disciples – not just better potential ministers.

- In some contexts, use of the term 'discipling' includes stress on disciplinary aspects of discipleship, and particular sets of values and patterns of behaviour inculcated on the basis of authority. Conformity of thought and obedience to these patterns plays a major part in 'discipling'.

  This is not what we mean by discipleship. While the root meaning of the word concerns discipline, Christian disciples are under the discipline of Christ. Jesus' educational method was not to offer dogmatic propositions for cognitive acceptance: he expected his followers to reflect on the demands he made and the allusive and often challenging content of his teaching, so as to take responsibility for their own response. In this sense Christian discipleship can be seen as self-discipline, rather than discipline imposed by those in authority within the Christian community.

Discipleship and EFD

In developing our recommendations we have recognized that discipleship is the calling of all Christians, and that those who respond to God's call to follow him share explicitly in his ministry and mission in the world. We want to ensure that learning connects with life experience and ministry and mission on the ground. We aim to create a framework which enables the agenda for education and training to be shaped by the context and needs of learners – in the world and not only in the Church.

5

Section 2

Goals, ethos and criteria

Aims for EDF programmes

We offer the following principles and criteria to enable the planning of EFD programmes. The aim of these programmes is to help students, individually and in community, to develop a habit of informed, critical and creative engagement with issues of faith, morality, discipleship, mission and ministry. Students should be expected to explore such issues in dialogue with the Bible and the Christian tradition, giving attention to the varied contexts of contemporary culture, the church in its cultural social and ecumenical settings, and their own daily life contexts, including work and church.

Our three churches already aspire to the convictions and principles expressed. During summer 2004 the task group consulted church adult education networks, DDOs and their denominational equivalents, and staff from theological colleges, courses and schemes. Responses showed that the underlying approaches, principles and goals are widely welcomed and seen as realistic. Comments received have been most helpful in honing and clarifying the framework for EFD criteria.

Underlying principles

The principles that govern our approach to EFD arise from our belief in the importance of the whole people of God and a commitment to life-long learning. These principles are:

i)   Every human being has a capacity for learning, which is part of what it means to be human;

ii)   Those who respond to God's call to follow him share explicitly in his mission in the world:

iii) Christian discipleship has both an individual and a corporate dimension, and is a collaborative as well as an individual response to Christ's call;

iv)   All God's people are called to discipleship; all are valuable; all are gifted;

v)   Communities and networks of learning are an invaluable resource to the Church;

vi)   The Church is resourced by the mutuality of learning between public ministers (lay and ordained) and the rest of the people of God;

vii) Learning designed to enhance discipleship needs to be rooted in understandings of the Christian tradition and the Bible;

viii) Learning is life-long.

6

We recognize that human institutions (such as the Church) have a tendency to create hierarchies in which some people are valued more than others. A role of education and training in the Church is to break those down rather than reinforce them.

Criteria:

(a) Outcomes

The expected outcomes of EFD programmes as a whole are that participating students should:

i)   Become more confident in faith, discipleship and understanding in relation to God, membership of the Church and engagement as Christians with the world;

ii)   Grow in their understanding of Christian identity, both within the Church community and in society at large;

iii) Be able to draw effectively on a solid grounding in knowledge and understanding of the Bible and the Christian tradition;

iv)   Be able to voice an understanding informed by Christian reflection and dialogue with others;

v)   Grow in their awareness of themselves and others;

vi)   Be open to the exploration of a variety of pathways in response to God's call to discipleship;

vii) Develop a deepening and sustainable life of prayer.

(b) Methodology

We recommend that regional partnerships develop programmes for EFD that meet the following criteria. Programmes should:

i)   Be open and work at being accessible to all;

ii)   Offer learning which connects with and values life experience;

iii) Offer opportunities for wider learning which build on experiences in the local church;

iv)   Incorporate learning processes that encourage corporate and collaborative as well as individual learning;

v)   Offer programmes which encourage people to take responsibility for their own learning and that of others as Christian disciples;

vi)   Offer programmes that provide opportunities for laity and those at different stages of preparing for public ministry to learn together, encouraging collaboration;

vii)   Provide education and training in a way which resources the mind, emotions and spirit;

viii) Offer education that is accessible to all personality types and takes into account different learning styles;

ix)   Offer opportunities so that participants who wish to gain accreditation of their work can obtain an HE award.

Applying the principles and criteria

This suggested framework of principles and criteria offers a key tool in ensuring that EFD programmes offered meet the proposed specifications.

It will be seen that the outcomes listed purposely bridge the division between 'Learning about Religion' and 'Learning from Religion' currently built into much curriculum planning in religious education at different levels.[1] Our aim is to ensure that both dimensions are incorporated and related throughout – in approach, in content addressed and in assessment process. This will help ensure a balance between introduction to subject content and reflection upon it. In terms of curriculum design the classification can be of help in ensuring that both dimensions are given weight.

Both outcomes and methodology are issues and concepts which are to be addressed throughout the programme, irrespective of module topic. The programme as a whole needs to ensure that all these criteria are met, though they are not intended as learning outcomes for individual modules (and not all will necessarily be a focus in every module). All individual modules offered under the programme will fulfil some of the criteria. In order to achieve the objectives of the EFD programme the full range of EFD criteria will need to be addressed in each region. As well as the varied subject matter of courses, a wide range of educational approaches will be needed. Appropriate educational methodology will make a significant contribution towards ensuring these goals are addressed. Wide use of educational approaches that incorporate collaborative learning processes will encourage the development of short-term learning communities, and of corporate as well as individual discipleship. Regional partnerships will need to develop appropriate ongoing processes of staff development and monitoring, and create learning materials designed to incorporate appropriate and varied educational process.

---

[1] E.g. QCA: The non-statutory national framework for religious education – 2004.

Section 3

EFD programmes

EFD and Education

We recognize the wide variety of learning opportunities offered by churches, and affirm the contribution that all different teaching and learning activities make towards developing the discipleship of Christ's followers. We are aware of the large demand for training at an access level – pre-HE level 1. Such courses often meet very local needs, and the remit of this task group has not included this work. We note, however, that these courses have not always been designed in ways that enable learning outcomes to be measured, and hope that in the future such courses will be developed in ways that build on current educational good practice in this area.

We recognize that the report *Formation for Ministry within a Learning Church* had in mind something more focused and structured than many parish/diocesan courses when it spoke of 'Education for Discipleship'. The guidance on EFD within the remit of the regional partnerships is based on the following understanding of 'education' in this context.

The 2003 report is concerned with theological education at quantifiable levels – specifically HE levels 1–4. While it would be unhelpful for regional partnerships to insist that programmes of EFD are only open to students registered as candidates for an award, we propose that all the discipleship education of a regional partnership should, at least in principle, be susceptible of accreditation at HE level 1 or above. While we recognize that most EFD will be offered initially at HE Level 1, we would encourage the possibility of some modules being accredited at higher levels, and note that some institutions already offer such opportunities.

Two things distinguish our understanding of 'Education for Discipleship' from the wide range of educational and formational activities in this area that take place in our churches:

- it is education delivered at a verifiable level (HE level one), whether or not it is formally validated and accredited;
- it has a high level of intentionality for those who participate: they must make conscious and informed choices in order to take part, because the want to take their discipleship development further.

Structure

We propose that regional partnerships ensure that EFD programmes are developed which offer a range of modules. It will then be possible for students to opt into single modules, or accumulate a range to gain an accredited award.

Existing training programmes use a variety of structures. We do not wish to exclude opportunities for regional partnerships to promote and develop existing provision that conforms to criteria listed in section 2 of this report. This may result in a 'mixed economy' of varying types of programme. While complete programmes that meet the criteria and achieve the outcomes listed may be offered, they should not be the only provision for EFD within a regional partnership, and modules that can be used separately need to be offered as well.

A modular pattern of adult education provision is increasingly familiar to many people, and this trend seems likely to develop in the light of the Government's five-year education strategy paper published in July 2004. This encourages 'Training programmes that allow adults to build up small units towards a full qualification, so as to fit round other commitments, and to be able to combine units in ways which meet their and their employers' needs'. [2]

We note that:

- A modular approach offers opportunities for potential candidates for ministerial selection to make use of differing parts of the programme. EFD programmes are not required to provide a core curriculum for those proceeding to ordination training.
- Experience in dioceses suggests some participants are more willing to sign up for short courses. Shorter modules can initially appear more accessible and appealing to those with varying experience and expectations of training programmes.
- A programme made up of a selection of modules can draw on some existing provision. Partners may offer some of their well-developed course material to EFD programmes of Regional partnerships.
- Modular programmes can in future enable Regional partnerships to add / change modules to meet specific needs.
- A modular programme can more easily offer opportunities for some learning alongside those on different learning programmes, e.g. Reader or lay ministry training.
- Some respondents to the consultation process have expressed concern that a modular programme results in the loss of a learning community. While recognizing potential drawbacks here, experience and research suggests that the appropriate use of collaborative learning methodologies can encourage the development of a corporate learning culture within a short time frame.
- A modular programme can also have potential disadvantages if a 'pick and mix' approach to learning leads to incoherence. Care will need to be taken to help students find appropriate pathways.

Academic accreditation

Formation for Ministry within a Learning Church recommends that the 'Education for Discipleship' initiative extend the provision of academically accredited courses, so that some programmes of this type are available throughout the church rather than only in some places as at present. (5.22, 2003 report). We propose that EFD programmes should be developed so that the programmes are accredited and that those who are registered on modules can be encouraged to attain credit points at HE level 1 or a qualification.

---

[2] Department of Education and Skills: Five -Year Strategy for Children and Learners, Chapter 7 – Adult Skills.

However, we believe that work for an academic qualification should be an option for participants, not a necessary requirement of attending EFD courses. (See section 5 below for possible current funding implications.)

In many situations the subject matter and content of courses at access level and HE level 1 are very similar. The difference is frequently in the assessment process and what the student is expected to demonstrate in terms of learning. We therefore encourage the provision of courses which include an optional 'HE level 1' assessment component, but which may also cater for other users.

Assessment processes need to be creative and varied. Excellent guidance is available on appropriate assessment processes involving group activity and varied ways in which evidence can be submitted (e.g. appendix 2, Part 3 Parameters of the curriculum and Post-ordination phase of IME). We strongly encourage the use of these approaches.

Provisions for churches' recognition and ensuring quality

In the 2003 report, one of the stated aims for EFD programmes is that such provision should be available throughout the country, and not only in certain areas.

The group has discussed the processes most likely to be appropriate to monitor this provision and its quality. One option would be for Education for Discipleship be subject to the Educational Validation Framework, which has the advantage that it is already, in some degree, ecumenical, with the Methodist and United Reformed Churches involved with the Educational Validation Panel and are represented on it (*Mission and Ministry* Appendix 3).

Being part of the Educational Validation process could imply being subject to inspection by the Church. This could be seen as giving a valuable signal as to how seriously the churches take lay education and training. But it might also be interpreted as introducing a bureaucratic level of control, which could stifle local initiative.

We suggest therefore that a **moderation process** be considered by the Church as a possible way to promote good practice and standards in EFD programmes. Discussion with those currently involved in Reader Moderation has convinced us that this is an appropriate model, which combines the advantages of central involvement and affirmation with recognition that within the specifications, local variations will be important.

These issues are to be addressed and clarified by a task group appointed to look at quality assurance and accountability, due to be convened during 2005.

Section 4

EFD and the churches

Existing provision and future partnership

As a new development, EFD offers an exciting opportunity for partnership between different providers within a regional partnership – including partner churches, dioceses and institutions. We believe it to be important that EFD provision is developed as a collaborative venture.

It has become clear during our consultations that much good work in lay theological and discipleship training is taking place, both through dioceses and churches and in what some institutions are already offering to interested lay participants. Not all training offered by Districts and Dioceses will necessarily be part of structured EFD programmes, although it has an important role to play in people's Christian growth. However, this vital work at local level falls outside the parameters of our remit.

Provision of academically accredited programmes is (with the exception of the national URC programme) geographically patchy. The EFD initiatives aim to provide opportunities for laity everywhere. Regional partnerships will be able to incorporate some of the good work currently offered (maybe with some adaptation) as part of the EFD provision if appropriate.

Churches: An example of current Church provision is the United Reformed Church's national programme of discipleship learning (Training for Learning and Serving, or TLS). This has involved some 600 adults since 1995. It emphasizes open access and within a common syllabus enables those who wish to gain Cert. HE credits through a validating university. The core of this programme has been a two-year Foundation course of biblical study with contemporary thematic application. National management has been important in enabling consistency of methodology and content to be maintained across regional delivery. A similar but shorter scheme has been available since 2003 where delivery is organised primarily by Districts on the basis of local demand.

Dioceses and Districts: Current lay training provision is very varied, in quantity, purpose and level (as explained in the 2003 report 5.22). Some diocesan training courses are accredited, and some modules could easily contribute to EFD programmes. Not all training offered by Districts and Dioceses will necessarily be part of EFD, as much important work done at present falls outside the parameters of our recommendations. This includes:

- some training work with congregations or groups in relation to their development and mission (including some work undertaken by specialists such as adult education advisers and Training and Development Officers);
- some practical training to develop skills used within churches (e.g. reading and leading intercessions);

- some training to develop locally recognized ministries, which vary from place to place according to local needs and strategy. It is possible, though, that some EFD modules could be part of the training used for these.

Training Institutions: Consultation with colleges, courses and schemes during summer 2004 revealed that several (courses especially) have welcomed non-ministerial 'associates' as student participants for many years. Others have run some short non-accredited 'open to all' courses. Schemes often offer some training for parish groups alongside their OLM candidates. Many institutions are looking forward to consolidating and developing some of this work in collaboration with other partners, and to producing modules that contribute to EFD provision within a regional partnership.

EFD and lay ministerial training

Formation for Ministry within a Learning Church (4.2) discusses whether the training of the clergy should take place, at least in part, alongside the education offered to lay people. It raises the possibility of models that emphasize the education of the whole people of God, and the potential of some training being shared between ministerial candidates 'and those with whom they will minister in the future so that mutual understanding and trust can be built up'.

The proposed modular structure of EFD lends itself to offering some training that can be shared between those with different callings. It is important in planning these to recognize that training people together will not in itself automatically ensure the development of mutual understanding and learning. Educational methodology needs to be carefully planned to ensure appropriate opportunities are provided for corporate interaction and collaborative learning.

In addition to the possibilities for potential candidates for ordination discussed below, some modules could be designed so they can be used by those involved in Reader / Preacher or other lay ministerial training – either pre or post authorization. Discussions with the Reader / Preacher implementation task group indicates possibilities here. Similarly, some modules could be appropriate for use by others involved (or hoping to be involved) in training for locally authorized ministries.

The role of EFD in discernment

The task group believes that the proposals for EFD laid out in this report will help fulfil the need for learning opportunities for those whose vocation to authorized ministry is being discerned.

The study of modules within an EFD programme, along with other activities suggested by a DDO or their denominational equivalents could help candidates to reflect through experience, reading and written work. EFD participation will provide evidence of developing learning and ability to reflect, and those responsible for preparing supporting papers will find this helpful. For other course participants, awareness of a sense of vocation may arise out of participation in EFD modules or programmes. Such people will continue to study and receive vocational support from DDOs / denominational officers.

DDOs and denominational equivalents will need to be fully integrated into the life of regional partnerships, working with adult educators and training institutions.

The participating denominations may make use of EFD provision in differing ways:

The United Reformed Church practice: The Training for Learning and Serving (TLS) programme referred to above is not part of recruitment or training for ordinands. However, during the TLS experience some participants become increasingly aware of a call to authorized ministry, stimulated and developed through the TLS emphasis on personal practice of systematic theological reflection.

Synod Moderators sometimes recommend that TLS is taken to gain necessary academic pre-requisites and to attain or demonstrate a measure of study discipline.

The Methodist experience: Methodist Foundation Training was introduced in 1999. It 'consists of programmes of training, education and formation for those judged to have a strong sense of Christian vocation to exercise their discipleship through some form of ordained or authorised lay ministry. A major purpose of such programmes shall be to enable the particular form of the vocation and the person's ability to exercise it to be more accurately discerned' (*The Constitutional Practice and Discipline of the Methodist Church*, S.O. 60). Training institutions deliver Foundation Training differently across the country, but all courses place a significant emphasis on the importance of theological reflection on placement experiences. Students are asked to fund themselves in part, to the tune of £1000, although in reality local churches or circuits often pay the required contribution for them.

After five years, it is apparent that Foundation Training has brought with it significant benefits, but has also raised some questions. It has been good to raise the level of theological education and self-confidence in ministry among those who are exploring their Christian vocation, and who may not necessarily go down the route of ordination; it has also been helpful to provide the church with concrete evidence to aid the discernment process when it comes to the point of candidating for ordained ministry. But there are questions about what is the most appropriate context for Foundation Training in order to facilitate genuine, open, vocational discernment. Is it appropriate that much of what is currently delivered happens in a context where ordination training is the prevailing culture? What are the implications of this for a learning Church? In addition, the question of exploring denominational identity has to be weighed against the advantages of working ecumenically. And the two-tiered selection process, first for entry into Foundation Training, and then candidating for ordained ministry, is not without problems. Hence the need for a review, which is currently underway, and which will, inevitably, take note of the Education for Discipleship report.

Anglican expectations: The report *Formation for Ministry within a Learning Church* suggests that prospective Anglican ordinands should be encouraged to engage with certificate level work in theology and obtain credits if they have not done so before, where this is appropriate for the candidate. At an earlier stage of discussion, some had expressed a hope that EFD might be able to provide a common starting place for the curriculum of training institutions, but this is not a statutory requirement, and ordinands will continue to arrive at training institutions with a wide range of starting points.

Many DDOs report the value of opportunities for potential candidates to engage with differing experiences of discipleship, church and issues of theology. EFD modules could assist candidates for ministry in this way, whether or not the study is used to gain academic credits. While candidates might attend courses and not be assessed, the task of doing assignments produces evidence to the candidate, DDO and Bishops' Advisers of the ability to engage with and benefit from study. For some, completion of certificate level might be helpful and appropriate to demonstrate their ability to study across a wide range of identified areas that include biblical knowledge and spirituality. Study with EFD could also provide some candidates with an appropriate and helpful educational referee.

Candidates for Anglican Reader or ordained ministry might build up a portfolio around the criteria for selection, which would help them to articulate their maturity of faith, self-awareness and knowledge. Modules which incorporate the following foci could also be of particular help to candidates:

- The role of particular ministries within a theology of the priesthood of all believers. Reader as well as Ordained ministry could be included.
- Appreciation of a particular denomination within a theology of the Church.

DDOs have noted that the proposed modular nature of EFD provision will assist flexibility and the opportunity to work appropriately with candidates with widely differing prior experiences. They also note that for the provision to be of most use, EFD modules should ideally provide regular opportunities for study to begin at different times throughout the year, and should not start only in September.

Section 5

EFD implementation

This section aims to address some of the practicalities of implementing the suggestions made by the EFD group.

Resources

A major issue that RTPs will need to address is how the costs of EDF programmes will be met and shared. The report *Formation for Ministry within a Learning Church* envisages EFD courses as part of the overall service the church offers and therefore 'At one level the Church should take the main responsibility for them in that they are a service to the Church as a whole . . . Thus the majority of the cost should be borne by the Church, with the corollary that the fees for individual modules should be modest' (5.27, 2003 report).

This suggestion of a modest contribution to fees from parishes or individuals (with possible diocesan bursaries, e.g. for potential ordinands) mirrors some current practice in relation to funding diocesan and church lay education courses. At present there are many places where a modest charge is made towards running costs such as production of course materials and tutors' expenses. However practice varies, and in other places courses are offered free, with the importance of lay training acknowledged by the ongoing overheads being paid for by the central church structures, district or diocese.

The 2003 report does not clarify the expected process of how national and local Churches will contribute 'the majority of the cost' of the development of EFD programmes. Elements of the report's proposals relating to training ordinands are, within the Church of England context, paid for by money allocated from Central General Synod funds under Vote 1 arrangements, and we note with some disappointment that at present EFD falls outside the scope of this funding stream. This funding will therefore need to be met by contributions (financially and 'in kind') form the many various partners within the RTPs.

We suggest that regions carry out a careful 'mapping' exercise, as suggested below, in order to note the various ways (including staffing) in which partners may be able to contribute to EFD. Limited research into current budgets has focused on courses that have already received academic accreditation, and which therefore experience the range of demands and expenses that such courses entail.

In relation to the development of EFD programmes, the following areas need to be considered:

Running costs

Current budgets for accredited lay development courses sometimes cover the production of course material and publicity, room hire, expenses incurred by tutors and frequently minimal gratuities in the form of book tokens! Administrative staff costs are sometimes included under these budgeted running costs, but in other places are hidden staff costs. Fees paid by course participants may, in some instances, make a contribution towards some of these costs. For example, in one diocese with a new accredited lay training programme, about £2k fees contribute to an £11k budget, which does not include staff costs.

Staff costs

Staff costs are frequently hidden in current budgets. Although in some cases administrative staff time is included in running costs, this is not always currently the case. Professional staff time of Adult Education Officers, Training Development Officers etc. can be considerable. This is especially so in the case of developing accredited courses. A typical example from one diocese estimated the equivalent of a half post in staff time to set up, develop and liaise with the accrediting body for their HE level 1 accreditation. Volunteer time (e.g. tutors, mentors, module writers) is also a hidden cost and makes a major contribution to the overall resource input. It will be important for regional partnerships to recognize expenses involved in ensuring volunteer teaching staff and assessors are resourced and trained appropriately, as this is usually an essential condition of academic accreditation.

Accreditation costs

Our research revealed an extremely varied picture of the financial arrangements that exist between accrediting institutions and churches running courses with academic accreditation. Partner Higher Education Institutions (HEIs) adopt different policies and the financial implications for the church vary enormously. One diocese discovered that funding arrangements resulted in a particular department offering a more favourable financial arrangement than another department in the same institution. Several course leaders have been surprised to discover others with funding arrangements that they had been told were impossible or not allowed. This suggests that it can be possible for anticipated costs to be substantially lower in this area if a regional partnership is willing to consider alternatives rather than insist on a particular provider.

Frequent changes of government funding policy and varying interpretations of current guidelines make it inappropriate to produce concrete guidelines. Currently (spring 2005) some limited support is often available for courses leading to recognized qualifications. But current guidelines do not fund 'leisure learning', so any such arrangements would not apply to those attending courses without seeking a qualification. Where funding from public money for accredited courses may be possible, practice in relation to HEFCE funding varies widely. We have discovered cases of one HEI treating a particular course development as 'budget neutral' while another similar institution charges a different diocese several thousand pounds annually for very similar provision.

Government policy has recently resulted in grant provision being heavily weighted towards the provision of basic literacy and numeracy. In one instance a diocesan lay education programme found it possible to access funds by working with an Education Department in a local HEI. The introduction of Foundation Degrees is an avenue being explored in at least one place, with the possibility of a partner HEI contributing to diocesan costs out of offering the diocese payment out of the government funding offered.

It is important to note that the costs involved are ongoing, and are not only one-off costs involved in setting up a course. Training staff with responsibilities for accredited courses have reported ongoing hidden staff costs, with a heavy time commitment involved in order to comply with quality and validation requirements – continuing institutional audits, collaborative reports, reviews of agreements, subject reviews, revalidations etc.

Implications for regional partnerships

The theology articulated in *Formation for Ministry within a Learning Church* affirms and encourages the development of the whole people of God. The report recommends the development of educational processes which further this, and the integrity of the enterprise requires that the needs of EFD programmes be addressed alongside other interests and demands on funding. It would not be acceptable for resources to be almost exclusively channelled towards the training of a limited group, as this would be inconsistent with the report's articulated principle of offering support for developing all people. It is clear from our limited research that it is unrealistic to expect accredited lay training courses or EFD to be completely 'budget neutral', though it is possible to find ways to lessen some of the costs some have feared. We encourage further carefully chosen and negotiated partnerships with HEIs that enable money from government funding streams to benefit these programmes.

Regional partnerships need to ensure that EFD resourcing is carefully audited, and look for appropriate ways to fund and contribute to this programme.

Mapping and review

Resources in the regions include a wealth of existing training programmes, some of which already work with many of the criteria suggested for EFD. It will be important for regional partnerships to monitor carefully existing provision to check whether they fit within the suggested frameworks of principles and outcomes. The same process will also need to be applied to any new programmes proposed. We use the term 'mapping' to describe this process.

Detailed specifications for EFD programmes will be the responsibility of regional partnerships, so this mapping will need to be carried out within each region. It will be important for the differing dimensions and issues noted in section 2 of this report to be looked at concurrently.

Groundwork for mapping

Our group has investigated and piloted a mapping process,[3] using the outcome and methodology criteria given in section 2 as a framework. We have recognized certain complexities, for example where modules are also to be used by trainee Readers/Preachers, other lay ministers and potential candidates for ordination. The EFD 'map' then overlaps with structured pathways to other ministries – each with its own emphasis and denominational requirements.

Three factors that need to be noted when undertaking this exercise are:

- Care needs to be taken with terminology, so that partners within a regional partnership use terminology in consistent ways.
- Imaginative and flexible (yet rigorous) methods of AP(E)L assessment will be required.

---

[3] The group has mapped the URC 'Training for Learning and Serving' Programme (TLS) and a Peterborough Diocesan Adult Education Programme against piloted Ethos and Goals. The Anglican Adult Education network was also invited to trial the process. The Readers/Lay Preachers Task Group has done a similar mapping between Methodist and Anglican requirements – with some attention to the Lichfield Certificate Course. These exercises have helped inform and hone our suggestions.

- EFD modules will need to be clearly described, in terms of content, educational process and assessment method. The topic title alone may do little to clarify this. It also needs to be clear where a module is introductory, and where it 'follows on', building on work done in other modules.

We recommend that mapping starts with the aims, principles and outcome and methodological criteria, set out above. Open questions can be used to enquire how in the curriculum these are met.

Another dimension of the mapping exercise will be to identify the availability of different resources across their regions, for example staff who have particular expertise in educational methodology or course construction.

Learning from the mapping exercise

A mapping exercise could lead practitioners in regions to find and share good practice.

Across EFD pathways or programmes it will be important that the outcome and knowledge goals all receive equal weight of treatment and attention. Our work has shown that currently some 'outcomes' and areas of study are catered for more frequently than others. For example, in our limited pilots we noted that areas of mission and engagement with the world are not always sufficiently well represented.

EFD modules will need to embrace a variety of learning methodologies if they are to meet requirements, especially those on accessibility. Different learning styles need to be catered for. We discovered that aspirations and good intentions in this area are sometimes more optimistic than the reality, and this area needs careful attention.

The identification of 'gaps' in provision will be an important task for regional partnerships. Mapping may also reveal some areas of potential overlap. Recognizing opportunities for sharing good practice and identifying areas where further work is needed will be important for regional partnerships as they plan to develop EFD provision and agree priorities for future development.

Illustrative programmes of Education for Discipleship

These illustrative examples are to be read in conjunction with the frameworks and criteria for EFD offered in section 2 of this report. They imagine different programmes that might be run in different regions (or across the same region), and reflect types of programmes that have been observed in practice.

The comments following each illustration aim to help illustrate the application of the frameworks, and draw attention to key principles and criteria most specifically addressed (or not) in each suggested programme. In practice, further information on the curriculum and proposed educational approaches would be needed in full submissions to expand outlines and enable a fuller check of the criteria. These might also clarify that other outcomes not obvious from brief module titles are being addressed.

In order to demonstrate appropriate academic rigour at the relevant level, a programme would also need to show that:

- the appropriate criteria are applied in the assessment of submitted work (demonstrated through independent assessment by an external examiner);
- the course content requires participants to engage with current issues and debate at an appropriate level;
- facilitators are theologically and educationally competent (through qualifications and participation in the provided training and development opportunities);
- provision is made for the monitoring, evaluation and on-going development of the programme in response to staff and student feedback.

None of the examples fully describes any existing programme, and some elements of imagination have been introduced into the scenarios below. However it may be helpful to note that each of the assessment packages described is currently used on a programme that is already accredited in the UK.

Example A

The programme

Everyone enrolled on the programme is required to take a core module in theological reflection before they take any of the other modules. The core module uses a variety of educational approaches, including material designed for home study using distance learning principles, input by facilitators, small-group discussion, project work and whole-class reflection to explore different ways in which Scripture, Christian tradition, reason, life experience and understanding of the world can be used to reflect theologically on issues faced by Christians today. Participants are helped to see how they are already reflecting theologically and how they can be become more skilful by reference in both private study and class work to case studies from their own life experience. An optional half day on study skills is included for those who wish it. The core module is assessed for all participants by means of syndicate-group presentations at the final session illustrating a variety of approaches to theological reflection on an issue chosen by each syndicate-group.

The programme is then arranged in four 'streams'; Understanding the Tradition, Engaging with the World, Relationships, and Walking with God. Each stream has a series of stand-alone modules using the variety of educational methodologies outlined above.

There are some basic modules which repeat from year to year (including introductions to Old and New Testaments and the Creeds, Ways of Praying, and Loving Self and Neighbour). The programme is reviewed every year to ensure that the modules take into account up-to-date thinking and address current issues, and the plan is that over time an increasing choice of modules will be introduced within each of the streams. The streams do not have to be followed in any particular order: participants can opt into an individual stream, though they would need to complete all to gain an award.

The modules are taught at a variety of centres across the region, and the individual work for home study is made available through E-learning.

All module leaders are expected to attend an initial training day on skills of working with adults and an annual refresher half day where they reflect on their experience of leading and learn more about contemporary understandings of adult education. The initial training highlights methods that enable learners to draw on their experience and engage critically with the tradition. The day involves action learning with people practising adult education in small groups.

The accredited assessment is at HE level 1. Validation has been negotiated with a university that has previously offered accreditation to several diocesan lay and ministerial training courses. Work presented for assessment is assessed in relation to the appropriate criteria for level and grade as set by the university, and the agreed assessment process includes both individual (70 per cent of marks) and group tasks (30 per cent of marks).

EFD Criteria

A. In relation to the EFD criteria set out above, this programme appears to be designed to secure the following outcomes:

- Become more confident in faith, discipleship and understanding in relation to God and to enable engagement with the world;

- Be able to draw effectively on a solid grounding in knowledge and understanding of the Bible and the Christian tradition;
- Be able to voice an understanding informed by Christian reflection and dialogue with others;
- Be open to the exploration of a variety of personal pathways in response to God's call to discipleship.

B. It meets the following EFD methodological criteria:

- It is open, and designed to be accessible to all.
- It offers learning which connects with and values life experience.
- It incorporates learning processes that encourage corporate and collaborative learning.
- It encourages people to take responsibility for their own learning and that of others.
- It models, facilitates and encourages a collaborative approach.
- It offers education that is accessible to all personality types and takes into account different learning styles.
- It offers opportunities for participants to gain a level 1 award.

On the basis of the information in this illustration, it looks likely that this programme forms the basis of a course that could meet the EFD criteria and fall within the proposed framework for EFD as understood in this report. It clearly bridges the divide between 'learning about religion' and 'learning from religion'. A range of methodological criteria are clearly met in the foundation module.

It would be necessary to check that the range of methodologies accessible to those with different learning styles is used in all streams, and that this criterion continues to be met as additional modules are added.

Example B

The programme

The focus of this programme is on the formational experience of discipleship for individuals. Although the programme has a significant collaborative element, the bulk of the curriculum is designed for individual learners to work on at home, following a pattern of structured learning. Learners sign up for a year's programme at a time, working primarily at home with printed materials, following a fairly traditional curriculum of theological study, but also participating in a weekly group meeting for three terms of 10 weeks in the year. Ideally groups are no more than 12 in number and the heart of each session is a period of theological reflection in which the group engages together. This is designed to enable group members to dialogue with each other in relation to an aspect of the Christian tradition in the light of their private study and daily experience. A different aspect of the Christian tradition is examined each term, so that learners acquire a solid content basis alongside skills of theological reflection. Each term there is the opportunity for learners to reflect specifically on their sense of call to follow Jesus and how that is being worked out in their daily life.

Accreditation is available for those who want to do written work, and this can build up towards a college certificate or diploma, but most of those following the programme opt not to do the work for accreditation, their primary motivation being to deepen their discipleship. Accreditation is through a Church college attached to a university. The programme as a whole lasts for four years, but the weekly group can comprise students from any of the years since the process of theological reflection, though informed by the subject matter in the rest of the curriculum, is not directly linked to it.

Tutors are required to attend a residential training weekend and need to attend annual days to sharpen their skills. The content of the private study is about the Christian tradition (Bible, Church History and Ethics) but the focus in each group session is on relating that to the learners' life experience and understanding of the world.

EFD Criteria

A. This programme appears to be designed to secure the following EFD outcomes:

- Become more confident in faith, discipleship and understanding in relation to God and to enable engagement with the world;
- Be able to draw effectively on a solid grounding in knowledge and understanding of the Bible and the Christian tradition;
- Be able to voice an understanding informed by Christian reflection and dialogue with others;
- Be open to the exploration of a variety of personal pathways in response to God's call to discipleship;
- Be able to draw effectively on a solid grounding in knowledge and understanding of the Bible and the Christian tradition.

B. It meets the following methodological criteria:

- It is open, and designed to be accessible (to anyone with the required skills in academic reading and writing).
- It offers learning which connects with and values life experience.
- It incorporates some learning processes that encourage corporate and collaborative learning.
- It encourages people to take responsibility for their own learning and that of others.
- To some extent it models, facilitates and encourages a collaborative approach (though it makes the assumption that learning is an essentially individual enterprise).
- It offers opportunities for participants to gain a level 1 award.

Because the programme is franchised from an overseas university (though it is modified for European use) there is little scope for the development of the curriculum through monitoring and evaluation. The programme is thus a less flexible and responsive example of what we mean by EFD than Example A.

This programme meets many (though not all) of the outcomes, principles and methodological criteria. It could be encouraged as making a contribution towards the provision of EFD as proposed in this report. However, there is little scope for development, and because it is non-modular and each year can only be taken as a whole it could not provide the sole EFD provision within a regional partnership.

Example C

The Programme

This programme consists of one- and two-year courses with a short Introductory Module including identification of preferred learning styles and the opportunity for optional written work assessment. The methodology includes residential weekends and home study units each with a local tutorial.

The basis of the two-year Foundation course (offered at Access Level 0 and Certificate Level 1) is contextual theology. In-depth Bible study on Old and New Testaments is accompanied by work on contemporary social, moral and ecclesial issues such as applied spirituality, the nature of society and community, public theology and ethics, suffering, the prophetic and institutional Church. It aims to offer learning opportunities to potential ministerial candidates and others seeking to develop their lay discipleship.

One-year courses can be taken at Access Level 0, Certificate Level 1 and Diploma Level 2. Titles embrace worship, prayer, care, inter-faith dialogue and creativity in worship. Foundation and the worship course are seen as a pathway for national accreditation as lay preachers, other one-year courses can be also be taken on a stand-alone basis.

The programme as a whole strongly emphasises theological reflection and self-appraisal, reinforced by set exercises in these areas. Throughout there is a thread of engagement with the missiological and prophetic role of the Church. The formational aspect is focused on an 'area of service' which students nominate for their discipleship context. All students have a Support Network, selected by them and for whom face-to-face training is provided.

Throughout the programme the use of non-textual assessment is encouraged. Local and weekend tutors are volunteers, drawn from the churches and trained and assessed by the Programme. Where students participate together at differing HE Levels all study together to an identical syllabus but assessment is multi-coded to provide appropriate assignments at the various levels. Promotion of the programme is based on open accessibility and the opportunity for self-development for the service of the gospel.

The accreditation has been negotiated with a local university, which has proved itself to be flexible in the ways it applies its criteria.

EFD Criteria

A. This programme appears to be designed to secure the following EFD outcomes:

- Become more confident in faith, discipleship and understanding in relation to God and to enable engagement with the world;
- Grow in understanding of Christian identity, both within the Church community and in society at large;
- Be able to draw effectively on a solid grounding in knowledge and understanding of the Bible and the Christian tradition;
- Be able to voice an understanding informed by Christian reflection and dialogue with others;
- Grow in self-awareness and awareness of others;
- Be open to the exploration of a variety of personal pathways in response to God's call to discipleship;

- Develop a deepening and sustainable life of prayer.

B. It appears to meet the following EFD methodological criteria:

- It is open, and designed to be accessible to all.
- It offers learning that connects with and values life experience.
- It offers opportunities for wider learning that build on experiences in the local church.
- It provides opportunities for laity and those at different stages of preparing for public ministry to learn together.
- It encourages people to take responsibility for their own learning and that of others;
- It models, facilitates and encourages a collaborative approach.
- It provides education and training in a way which resources the mind, emotions and spirit.
- It offers opportunities for participants to gain a level 1 award.

It appears likely that this programme forms the basis of a course that could meet the EFD criteria and fall within the proposed framework for EFD as understood in this report. It clearly bridges the divide between 'learning about religion' and 'learning from religion'. A range of methodological criteria are clearly met. Some details would need to be checked in a more detailed review – for example it would be necessary to check that approaches do cater for a full range of learning styles, that there are collaborative learning opportunities for all students, and that the 'non-textual assessment' that is encouraged does in practice offer scope for a range of practices, possibly including group assessments.

Example D

The Programme

This programme has been developed in consultation with a local university and is offered across the region. Accreditation is offered at levels 1 and 2, and it is understood that the purpose of participation is to gain HE credits towards an academic award. The course is entitled 'Theology for the Contemporary Christian'. The publicity indicates that the objective is to equip lay Christians with a solid grasp of current academic theological debate that will provide them with a foundation of theological understanding and familiarity with contemporary issues. It is suggested that the programme will be particularly helpful to those who preach or teach as well as those who want to familiarize themselves with current issues in theology or who want to study the subject for its own sake and for the love of learning.

Teaching is primarily by means of lectures and academic seminars, by university and college staff whose existing academic qualifications are already recognized by the university. The programme sets out to offer the highest quality teaching to lay Christians and consists of a series of modules including: Introduction to the Old Testament; Introduction to the New Testament; New Testament Greek; Principles of Christian Theology; Church History from the early Church to the Reformation; Church History from the Reformation till Vatican 2; Philosophy of Religion; Christian Ethics. To broaden the appeal of the programme, modules on Feminist Readings of the Bible and Modernism, Post-modernism and Culture are also included.

The sessions comprise lectures followed by questions, with occasional seminars at which students present short papers reflecting their own work, which are discussed in a peer group, supervised by a tutor. Work submitted for accreditation is in the form of essays. Those doing the course are expected to be able to write competently, to reference their work accurately and to present bibliographies correctly.

Since experienced full-time lecturers undertake the teaching, no additional staff training is considered necessary.

EFD Criteria

A. This programme appears to be designed to meet the following EFD outcomes:

- Be able to voice an understanding informed by Christian reflection and dialogue with others;
- Be able to draw effectively on a solid grounding in knowledge and understanding of the Bible and the Christian tradition.

B. It appears to meet the following EFD methodological criteria:

- It is open, and designed to be accessible to all.
- It offers opportunities for wider learning that build on experiences in the local church.
- It provides opportunities for laity and those at different stages of preparing for public ministry to learn together.
- It encourages people to take responsibility for their own learning and that of others;

- It offers opportunities so that participants who wish to gain accreditation of their work can obtain a level 1 award.

This programme performs a valid and valuable function and fulfils some of the EFD criteria. However it appears unlikely that it would fall within the proposed framework for EFD as understood in this report. Its intended outcomes clearly encourage 'learning about religion' and confidence in this area, but it is not clear that it also specifically aims to focus on 'learning from religion' or how it promotes an understanding of engagement as Christians with the world. It does not at present demonstrate ways in which it would meet the full range of methodological criteria.

- It offers opportunities so that participants who wish to gain accreditation of their work can obtain a level 1 award.

Example E

The Programme

Programme E has been developed by a denominational college in a region working in conjunction with a national adult education office. In consultation with other partners across the region, aspects of denominational bias have been taken out of the programme and it has been adopted as one of three programmes offered across the region.

The programme is based on distance learning materials, which are delivered in one of a number of ways.

- Modules are taught at the residential college, which is based in the largest city in the region for those within easy travelling distance. Some of these are attended by residential students, some of whom are training for ordination.
- Modules are taught in local groups by local tutors. The tutors are appointed by the local regional partner which takes responsibility for their training and support following guidelines laid down by the college.
- Modules are studied through E-learning using a chat-room format moderated by a supervisory tutor.

Learners attend a day and a residential weekend each year. The days and weekends are held in three centres across the region, chosen for their access to public transport and good road links.

The programme consists of three access level units, which can lead on to a two-year foundational course. The foundation course can be done without accreditation or with 80 credits at level 1. Further one year units with a practical emphasis and the option of 40 credits at level 1 are being developed in consultation with all the partners in the region to make sure that they meet actual needs.

The access level units are called 'Word and World', 'Wonder and World' and 'Ways in the World'. The aims of the three units are respectively to help learners:

- find their way around the Bible in relation to the context of the world in which it was produced and our own world;
- talk about God in relation to their experience of the world and their own spirituality;
- develop skills in reading the world through Christian eyes, and discerning their vocation as Christians in response.

The foundational course builds on these three areas in more depth. Each session starts with the experience of the learners, introduces an aspect of Christian theology and helps learners to make connections between the two. The work for accreditation involves reflection on experience as well as further reading and analysis. By the end of the two years learners have encountered some major aspects of Biblical theology, Christian believing, Christian history and Christian ethics.

The guidelines for tutor training focus on skills in helping learners develop reflective practice and learn collaboratively. Learners are asked to keep a learning journal throughout the programme in which they are asked to respond to questions like: What has struck me? What has challenged me? What has led me to think differently? What difference will this make to my personal life, my 'work' context, my community, my church?

The programme is accredited by a university, which lies outside the region, but which has been proactive in developing links with regional partners across the country and has extensive experience of accrediting experience based theological courses.

EFD Criteria

A. This programme appears to be designed to secure the following EFD outcomes:

- Become more confident in faith, discipleship and understanding in relation to God and to enable engagement with the world;
- Grow in understanding of Christian identity, both within the Church community and in society at large;
- Be able to draw effectively on a solid grounding in knowledge and understanding of the Bible and the Christian tradition;
- Be able to voice an understanding informed by Christian reflection and dialogue with others;
- Be open to the exploration of a variety of personal pathways in response to God's call to discipleship;
- Grow in self-awareness and awareness of others.

B. It appears to meet the following EFD methodological criteria:

- It is open, and designed to be accessible to all.
- It offers learning which connects with and values life experience.
- It offers opportunities for wider learning that build on experiences in the local church.
- It encourages people to take responsibility for their own learning and that of others.
- It models, facilitates and encourages a collaborative approach.
- It offers education that is accessible to all personality types and takes into account different learning styles.
- It offers opportunities for participants to gain a level 1 award.

On the basis of the information in this illustration, it looks likely that this programme could meet the EFD criteria and fall within the proposed framework for EFD as understood in this report. It clearly bridges the divide between 'learning about religion' and 'learning from religion'. A range of methodological criteria are met, though it would be necessary to check carefully that all three alternative modes of delivery provide opportunities for laity and those at different stages of preparation for ministry to work together, and that each incorporates learning processes that encourage corporate and collaborative learning.

Part 2

A vision for good practice in Reader/Preacher training

A report of the implementation task group

Section 1

Starting points

The goals of *Formation for Ministry within a Learning Church*

Training in context

Formation for Ministry within in a Learning Church (2003) placed its review of ministerial education and formation of the clergy in the context of 'the Church's total provision for ministerial training, lay training and formal lay adult education (*Formation for Ministry within in a Learning Church,* Summary, p. 2). The Reader Task Group was formed to explore further one part of that broader context. Our focus has been on the training of Readers, but throughout we have been mindful of how that training needs to relate well to lay education and to training for ordained ministry. The original report advocates such a relationship between these strands of education and training.

Partnerships

Regional partnerships will be able to draw together people from 'diocesan training establishments, theological colleges and courses in collaboration both with other churches and UK higher education' (Summary, p. 12). The Reader Task Group itself has been an expression of such partnerships. Our proposals in this 'Vision for good practice' give expression to the report's purposes for regional partnerships:

- To contribute to the initial training of Readers and other lay ministers;·
- To contribute to continuing ministerial education for all ministries;
- To contribute to the formal theological education of the laity.

Learning pathways

As people move within and across strands of education and training, so there is a need that their previous learning and experience is acknowledged in a way that enables fresh learning and the development of new skills. The Reader Task Group encourages open access to training provision which invites students to enrich their discipleship and explore their calling to ministry. We appreciate also that for some, the accreditation of courses by higher education will offer rigour and recognition to their learning and development. There is a creative tension here for regional partnerships to explore with training providers in order to offer appropriate learning pathways for all students.

Reader Task Group aim

The aim of the Reader Task Group has been to use the goals of the original report that impinge on Reader training to produce 'A vision for good practice' which clarifies the advantages of working in partnerships:

- with other dioceses;
- with other churches;
- with ministerial training institutions;
- with Higher Education (HE) institutions.

That aim remains, strengthened by the responses from dioceses and partner churches during the consultation period in early 2005. The Reader Task Group thanks all who contributed to that consultation. The report has been welcomed by most, so alterations have been minor. Even so, the responses have caused us to discuss issues further. Among the issues raised have been:

- the encouragement of a single training programme (with flexibility) for each regional partnership;
- the degree of similarity and difference between Reader and Preacher roles;
- issues of cost that regional partnerships will need to face;
- accreditation issues for students, regional partnerships and partner churches.

Other matters raised by the consultation have also been heeded. This revised report seeks to clarify these issues at appropriate points and begins by clarifying the implications for its 'Vision for good practice' that stem from the Reader Task Group aim.

Implications

Think regionally

Members of the Reader Task Group have come from several dioceses and from the Methodist Church and the United Reformed Church. We have recognized that all of us have had to adjust our perspectives (diocesan and national) to a new regional focus. We have had to take account of those different, apparently conflicting perspectives and interests, but increasingly we have found advantages in thinking regionally. These advantages include:

- effective use of resources, especially human resources;
- a larger client group when developing a working relationship with an accrediting body;
- efficient and effective training provision in terms of location of centres, viability of group sizes and quality of teaching and assessment;
- keeping open appropriate opportunities for Readers/Preachers to train alongside ordinands and/or other lay people.

Think ecumenically

The Methodist Church and the United Reformed Church have been partners throughout the review process. The Reader Task Group's ecumenical basis has been helped by:

- the similarity between the numbers of Church of England Readers in training and Preachers in training in the partner churches;
- the similarity between all three denominations in objectives for Reader/Preacher training;

- the similarities of role for Readers and Preachers that people in these ministries acknowledge already;
- the similar vision that all three churches have for the further development of Reader/Preacher roles.

These similarities came as something of a surprise to us. They encouraged us to be equal partners in the process and to propose a single set of guidelines for the training of Readers and Preachers. We see value in members of RTPs working ecumenically as equal partners and enabling regional provision for Readers, Local Preachers and Lay Preachers to train together. All these considerations have led us to use the phrase Reader/Preacher in this paper.

The high degree of common ground for Readers/Preachers has helped us frame an ecumenical training specification. Within that framework we specify essential learning outcomes to help clarify our goals for Readers/Preachers. There is still some work for partner churches to do to amplify these outcomes to indicate how Reader/Preacher training:

- is properly related to ordination training;
- is distinct from ordination training;
- has a sense of progression through initial training and through continuing development.

Think Higher Education

At present, there is no common approach to the accreditation of Reader/Preacher training across dioceses or across denominations. We recommend the accreditation of training provision by a Higher Education (HE) institution because it gives an assurance of quality in terms of:

- the provision itself;
- the assessment of individual students;
- consistency in provision across regions.

Open access to accredited training programmes demands that delivery is sensitive and responsive to students' individual needs. Some students, including those who are possibly looking towards ordination, will need accreditation not only of their Reader/Preacher training, but also of their previous learning and experience. It will be essential for each regional partnership to have good working relationships with an HE institution if training provision is to meet:

- the training needs of individuals;
- the training requirements of the denominations;
- the accreditation requirements of an HE institution.

The goals set out in *Formation for Ministry within a Learning Church* as outlined here present an exciting and challenging opportunity to all involved in Reader/Preacher training. In this 'Vision for good practice' we paint a picture with broad brush strokes, inviting others to develop works of art that enrich their own situations. To that end, we:

- provide regional partnerships with a single, yet flexible, specification for Reader/Preacher training (in Section 2);
- outline the value of playing a full part in a regional partnership (in Section 3);
- offer a possible way of supporting the continuing development of Readers/Preachers (in Section 4);
- consider how some are already taking steps towards this 'Vision' and how denominational partners envisage transition management (in Section 5).

Section 2

Training specifications

A national and ecumenical specification for the education and training of Readers/Preachers

Context of this specification

All our three churches, the Church of England, the Methodist Church and the United Reformed Church, have accredited lay ministries which involve leading worship and preaching. Often people carrying out these roles also have a teaching ministry, for example in leading house groups or preparing people for church membership. In recent years these ministries have had an increasing role in the sacraments of the Church – with particular authorization as appropriate. All these ministries require pastoral understanding and pastoral sensitivity.

It has been encouraging to note how similar in practice are the ministries of Readers in the Church of England, Lay Preachers in the United Reformed Church and Local Preachers in the Methodist Church. Readers and preachers used to be the only authorized lay ministries, but now there is greater multiplicity of lay ministries, varying from church to church. There is every sign that this trend will continue as we explore new expressions of being Church in practice and structure. This specification seeks to embrace such diversity and to prepare for emerging ministries rather than simply perpetuating existing forms of ministries.

Scope of this specification

Our purpose has been to provide Church-wide criteria for Reader/Preacher training which are common to all three denominations. The criteria are for use by regional partnerships as they devise ecumenical training for Readers/Preachers. They are also a means whereby all three denominations together can measure the quality of a regional partnership's proposed education and training provision and its subsequent implementation.

It is recognized that the decision to admit a person to Reader/Preacher ministry rests with their denomination and not with a regional partnership.

This specification has to be more than merely a specification for the initial training of Readers/Preachers. The original report of 2003 is clear that initial training is part of a continuum of education and training which draws on previous experience and learning. It is also clear that, whether people remain as Preachers/Readers or move into another kind of ministry, they need to continue to learn and develop. There is therefore an expectation that regional partnerships will integrate provision for Education for Discipleship and Continuing Ministerial Education with Reader/Preacher training. Our concern is for the learners, so that their previous experience and learning is valued and built on, and that they continue to grow as their ministries develop.

Underlying principles of this specification

Essential principles for Reader/Preacher education and training are:

- to make maximum use of **ecumenical** resources and opportunities, to appreciate the gifts and strengths of our ecumenical partners and to value our own tradition;
- to promote and reflect on **collaborative** working, at all levels, whether it be:

  o ecumenical;
  o within the education and training provision itself;
  o among the learners;
  o in local situations;
  o between ministries;
  o with congregations (e.g. shared planning, participation in worship);

- to promote an **enabling** ministry which fosters learning and growth

  o within the education and training provision itself;
  o among the learners;
  o in local situations and with congregations;

- to provide learning opportunities **accessible** to the broadest possible range of people:

  o encouraging imaginative ways of acknowledging previous experience and learning;
  o offering introductory preparation and support (e.g. through an Education for Discipleship programme, taster courses and/or use of learning advisers);
  o stretching people beyond their current capabilities by including depth as well as breadth;
  o making learning fun;
  o assessing imaginatively rather than by examination;
  o ensuring that no one testing their call to Reader/Preacher ministry is denied access for financial reasons;

- to provide **reflective** learning opportunities by:

  o requiring regular self-appraisal by learners;
  o requiring theological reflection on the everyday, current affairs, contemporary culture;
  o relating academic theology, Bible study and the here-and-now.

Education and training framework

The training of Readers/Preachers involves Knowledge and Understanding, Competence and Conviction:

While each area is important in itself, formation occurs in their dynamic interaction.

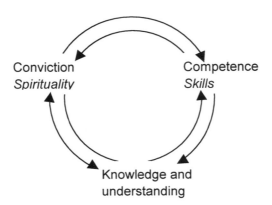

Together, in balance, they shape the life and ministry of a Preacher/Reader.

1   Knowledge and understanding

In order to contribute to the ministry of the Church and to witness to the faith in the world, it is essential that Readers/Preachers acquire good grounding in theology and Christian doctrine. Essential learning outcomes are:

A working knowledge of the Bible

- understanding different views about the truth and authority of the Bible and its continuing application today, and coming to a reasoned, reflective commitment to a personal view;
- engaging with Bible passages for oneself;

- exploring the methods and insights of biblical criticism and interpretation and showing their relevance for contemporary worship, preaching and mission.

A basic understanding of Christian doctrine

- reflecting on major statements of faith held by Christians, and demonstrating their application to contemporary issues;
- reflecting on the traditions and histories of the Church, denominational emphases and expectations of Readers/Preachers;
- reflecting on the nature of the Church and its mission.

An exploration and appreciation of the theology of worship, the diversity of worship and liturgy in our denominations and their significance for the contemporary Church;

- recognizing the pattern of the Church Year, theological themes and wide use of the Bible in the Revised Common Lectionary;
- exploring traditional and contemporary expressions of spirituality in the Christian Church and beyond.

Critical reflection on issues

- considering contemporary theological issues;
- reflecting theologically on contemporary moral, ethical and social justice issues;
- evaluating ways that theology might be expressed to people outside the Church.

2   Competence

In order to encourage lively, inclusive, worshipping communities in a variety of contexts, it is essential that Readers/Preachers acquire skills in leading worship, in preaching, in enabling learning, communication and mission and in pastoral sensitivity. Essential learning outcomes are:

Worship-leading skills

In order to empower people to worship within the church and outside of it (workplace, home etc.), it is essential that training for worship leading develops skills in:

- reading the Bible clearly and in an appropriate manner;
- leading prayers and meditations with sensitivity;
- the use of denominational and other liturgical resources;
- choosing appropriate hymns / songs;
- working collaboratively with worship leaders, musicians and others;
- using the arts and new technology (as appropriate and as available);
- devising and leading a variety of services such as all-age worship;
- evaluating what has been prepared against accepted liturgies.

Preaching skills

In order to proclaim (in a variety of contexts) the challenging and comforting good news of God's love in Christ, it is essential that training for preaching develops skills in:

- handling biblical passages appropriately and imaginatively;
- setting Bible passages and stories in their wider context;
- using commentaries and other tools;
- relating Bible exegesis and contemporary experience;
- articulating faith and theology in an informed and accessible way;

- developing a variety of styles of preaching appropriate to different groups and different settings, including the use of the arts and new technology (as appropriate and as available);
- choosing and organizing other activities that could function as a sermon, including collaborative ventures;
- addressing a range of moral and ethical issues.

Skills to enable learning, communication and mission

In order to help people communicate faith in the Church and in the world, it is essential that Readers/Preachers develop skills in:

- gauging where people are and how they might develop;
- appreciating that people learn in a variety of ways;
- using varied and appropriate styles that help people learn;
- fostering collaborative ways of working and learning;
- evaluating how well people have learned / grown.

Pastoral skills

In order to develop pastoral sensitivity in a variety of settings, it is essential that Readers/Preachers develop skills in:

- gauging where people are emotionally and spiritually;
- listening without being judgemental;
- managing confidentiality;
- handling conflict;
- encouraging others in discipleship, ministry and faith-sharing.

3. Conviction and spirituality

Formation

In order to nurture their Christian life, it is essential that Readers/Preachers are meeting with God as they continue to test their calling throughout their training and ministry. Who they are, as people; their spirituality, attitudes, qualities and maturity, in their home church community and in the wider world, are as important as their knowledge and competence.

To nurture their Christian life and ministry, it is essential that Readers/Preachers:

- are developing, reflecting on and evaluating their personal discipline of prayer, worship and thoughtful study of the Bible;
- are aware of, and are exploring the resources available for spiritual growth;
- are reflecting on God in other experiences;
- explore their understanding of, and participation in God's mission;
- appreciate the spirituality of their own and others' traditions (ecclesial, cultural, etc.);
- experience, and reflect on, the worship and spiritual life of different congregations.

Continuing development

Continuing development is a fresh exploration of new areas as well as a refreshing and up-dating of existing knowledge, skills and spirituality. The underlying principles of this specification (ecumenical, collaborative, enabling, accessible, reflective) and the overlap and balance of Knowledge, Competence and Conviction are equally essential in the devising of continuing development provision.

The ideal for Continuing Development provision is:

- ecumenical, centrally agreed resource materials with study guides;
- regional activities, resources and events;
- scope for local ecumenical support;
- annual points of completion and achievement for each individual's development portfolio;
- an overlap between provision of continuing development for Readers/Preachers and CME;
- cost-effective, funded as much as possible by denominations.

One possible approach to this provision is outlined in section 4 of this report.

How initial training and continuing development are delivered

It is essential that the ways in which Reader/Preacher training (initial training and continuing development) is delivered reflect the underlying principles (ecumenical, collaborative, enabling, accessible, reflective). Therefore, there is an expectation that the teaching and tutoring model these qualities and demonstrate the competences expected of Readers/Preachers.

Other essential features are:

- the acknowledgement, valuing and use of each learner's previous experience and learning;
- an appropriate mix of input and experiential work;
- an appropriate mix of individual and group settings;
- an appropriate range of learning methods (e.g. distance learning, locally supported learning, seminar work, computer interactive working, practical experience);
- imagination, creativity and fun;
- assessment which is moderated to the satisfaction of the participating denominations;
- provision of an HE accredited training programme, which allows students engaging in a common programme either to work for HE credits or not;
- reflection on and evaluation of the learning experience by learners, teachers, tutors and mentors.

Much of this specification is relevant to the formation of other lay ministries and, indeed, ordained ministries. We have aimed to express it in ways that encourage cross-referencing, further development and appropriate application. Our main sources for this section have been *Reader Ministry and Training 2000 and Beyond*, *What makes a Local Preacher?* and TLS 2003-4 Course Handbooks.

Section 3

Partnership to deliver the training specification

Each regional partnership will need to explore a way forward that works in its own set of circumstances as it responds to the Training Specification. Regional partnerships will differ in size, geography, the communities they serve and the traditions of the partner institutions themselves.

In terms of Reader/Preacher training, each regional partnership will need to address many issues, some of which are outlined here.

One programme for the region

At present, each diocese has its own training scheme for Readers which responds to the local socio-economic needs, ministry needs and each student's needs. In a few cases, two or more dioceses already share a common course. Many courses are already accredited by an HE institution. Methodist Local Preachers and United Reformed Church Lay Preachers have national schemes of training (using open learning approaches). There are three pilot schemes where Readers and Local Preachers share the same training course. Despite this varied provision, there is already some movement drawing dioceses and denominations closer together.

The partners in an RTP bring considerable expertise in designing and delivering high quality Reader/Preacher training. In order to draw closer together regionally, this wealth of expertise and experience should inform and enrich a region's training programme. Partners will need to recognize and value the merits (often hard won) of each other's existing provision. Equally, partners will need to accept some unravelling of existing provision (national and diocesan) in order to weave a new regional training programme. We have discovered these features of partnership in the Reader Task Group while working on what has become a single Training Specification.

. . . with flexibility

The ready way in which we formulated a single Specification leads us to recommend movement towards a single training programme for each region. The Specification itself has room for manoeuvre and flexibility, so it embraces the possibility of variation to meet denominational needs and local circumstances within one programme. Examples of appropriate variations could include: urban, rural and ethnic contexts and commonalities with training for other lay ministries. Thus there will need to be 'variations on the theme', but also there will be plenty of opportunities for dioceses and denominations to unite with one voice. We believe that the adoption of a single, flexible training programme for Readers/Preachers in a region has the following advantages:

- The sharing of the task can reduce staff time needed to set up and review training provision.
- One partnership with a larger number of students can attract an HE institution to join the partnership.
- Teaching staff and tutors can be used more efficiently and effectively.
- Students can have more colleagues to support and encourage their own learning.
- There can be wider opportunities for learning, training and development within existing administration and staffing costs.
- There is scope to develop Reader/Preacher ministries as Partners learn from each other's contexts, forms (and applications) of ministry and exercise of ministry education.

All training in all regions will need to meet the Training Specification. As each region explores how best to adopt the specification, the goal should be to work towards a single training programme with a strong common core and appropriate variation which enables flexible approaches to local delivery that serve well Readers/Preachers in training.

Programme delivery

At present, diocesan and other denominational boundaries, training centres and tutor support provision may not always relate well to centres of population or to work / leisure travelling patterns. A review of how and where training is offered across a region can enable partners to:

- think afresh about training programme delivery, including the use of open learning methods and new technology (Internet, DVD, CD-ROM, telephone conferencing etc.) to make training opportunities more accessible and flexible;
- check what approaches to delivery may be offered within a region;
- reconsider suitability of existing places for programme delivery (including diocesan centres and colleges) and make appropriate and imaginative changes;
- explore ways to take training programme delivery to where students are (rather than vice versa).

Learning together

At present, some Reader/Preacher training is carried out alongside training of other people, for example those taking part in Education for Discipleship. Some Readers/Preachers train alongside ordinands for part of their training (at times on a regional ordination course). Some have diocesan schemes where Readers and Ordained Local Ministers are trained together.

We encourage regional partnerships in such developments, not only in initial training but also in their support for continuing development of Readers/Preachers because they:

- allow a sharing of ideas between Readers/Preachers, other lay people and those who are to become ordained ministers;
- encourage better understanding of different perspectives and roles in the local church setting;
- offer considerable scope for ecumenical benefits, especially in areas where students and teachers/tutors in individual denominations are few and far between.

Training with others is particularly helpful when it promotes collaborative ministry and prepares Readers/Preachers for collaborative ministry. Learning together with candidates for other ministries (lay and ordained) is not always appropriate, however, so consideration will need to be given to how far it is desirable and/or possible. An appropriate mix of training together and ministry-specific training should be a feature of the flexibility of a single regional training programme.

Modular approach

Higher Education institutions are familiar with modular approaches to training provision, so a regional partnership may choose a modular approach. Where this is the case, we would encourage a cross-referencing of modules so that what is learned in one module is not hermetically sealed from what is learned in others. For a modular programme to be of most value for Reader/Preacher purposes, it should enable;

- important areas of learning to be explored in more depth in other contexts (e.g. when revisiting an area of study and applying it);
- connections to be made to promote integrated learning and Reader formation;
- a coherent whole in the overall pattern of training that properly equips Readers/Preachers for their ministry.

When using a modular approach, it is also important that all permutations of modules combine in a way that meets the Training Specification.

Resources

The recruitment of teachers, tutors and assessors is becoming increasingly difficult in all our churches. Those who are currently engaged in aspects of Reader/Preacher training are often working with quite small numbers of students. A regional approach opens up the possibility of more effective use of teachers and tutors. It allows training providers to access the wealth of knowledge and skills brought by teachers and tutors across the region. Also, it enables better provision of support for and development of teachers and tutors than is currently available in any of our denominations.

It is important that students, teachers and tutors should have access to extensive and up-to-date library facilities. We invite regional partnerships to:

- carry out an audit of existing resources (not just books and journals, but also audio, visual, creative arts, IT etc.) within the region;
- review provision of resources so that it meets the needs of students, teachers and tutors in terms of content and location;
- check on how accessible resources are to those who need them and, if necessary, negotiate access;
- ensure that students know what resources are available and how they can access them.

Quality

The three partner churches will need assurance that all Reader/Preacher training programmes are appropriate for the purposes the churches specify and of a good standard. To that end, regional partnerships will need to demonstrate how any student's training is guided and directed so that it:

- equips them for the ministry of a Reader/Preacher as specified by each of the partner churches and dioceses;
- fulfils the ecumenical training specification in this report;
- takes account of each student's prior experience and learning;
- enables students who move from one part of the country to another to continue their training and development as Readers/Preachers.

In order to ensure that formational purposes are served effectively by Reader/Preacher training programmes and given consistent oversight by partner churches, we recommend the establishment of a single ecumenical process for quality and accountability (rather than having separate processes for each partner church). The form of this process will need to be worked out by our churches following the work of the Hind task group on quality and accountability due to report in 2006.

Accreditation

We anticipate that a training programme would develop in students the kinds of skills and approaches to learning that are associated with HE level 1 and 2. We believe that the time has come for all Reader/Preacher training programmes to be accredited by an HE institution. As we stated in section 1, there are advantages to sponsors and to students. Accreditation enables:

- assurance that the programme is of an appropriate educational standard;
- approaches to learning associated with HE levels 1 and 2 which equip people well for Reader/Preacher ministry;
- assurance that the assessment of individual students is consistent, thorough and fair;
- consistency of education and training provision across regions;
- access to an HE institution's resources and expertise;
- individual students to gain HE credits for reasons which could be personal, work-related or vocational.

Our emphasis is on the educational accreditation of training programmes. This keeps options open for individual students to gauge whether it is appropriate or not for them to work towards gaining HE credits.

In developing a Reader/Preacher programme, regional partnerships will need to note the following points:

- An existing HE certificate course will not necessarily meet the initial training needs of Readers/Preachers. The specification in this paper clarifies what is expected by partner denominations of Reader/ Preacher training.
- Training programmes should be comprehensive, satisfying all the requirements of the Training Specification and catering for students who are seeking to earn HE credits as well as those who are not. The gaining of HE credits is not the prime aim of Reader/Preacher training. However, we owe it to students to enable them to gain credits if they so wish.
- Training programmes should be cost-effective. The delivery and administration of any programme has costs. The real costs of current provision (how they are paid for and by whom) can be overlooked all too easily. However, there is evidence already that when delivery, administration and accreditation of a training programme is developed and negotiated with a sympathetic HE institution, many benefits accrue. Imaginative training

can go hand-in-hand with provision that is not only cost-effective but also takes full advantage of regional and current financial opportunities.

- Training programmes should integrate academic and practical training. We do not recommend a model where an HE-accredited course covers only academic learning, leaving a church partner to 'add-on' the practical elements of training.

Regional partnerships will benefit from the experience of gaining accreditation from institutions of Higher Education which is available from ministerial training institutions and some Reader/Preacher training programmes.

As a result of these considerations, for Reader/Preacher training (and, indeed, for other training) it will be important for regional partnerships to consider:

- how they select an appropriate HE partner;
- how to exercise the client role with an HE partner;
- how to enable easy day-to-day liaison with HE partner;
- how to establish and exercise an educational monitoring process.

Section 4

Continuing development

A suggested strategy to support the continuing development of lay and ordained preachers and worship leaders.

Continuing development can be a product of:

- individual activity
- small group (2–3 people) activity (denominational or ecumenical)
- larger group activity (denominational or ecumenical)

all at a very local level.

Continuing development can also be supported by:

- regional events (denominational or ecumenical)
- resources in regional libraries (at theological resource centres).

At present, denominations are not providing training resources for continuing development to the same extent that they resource initial training. In some denominations, evidence of continuing development is necessary for a Reader/Preacher to continue serving in that ministry, but even there, appropriate resources are not always specified. The following ecumenical strategy could be a helpful way forward:

A small ecumenical group to:

1   draw up a specification for resource materials that:
- promote use of the support mechanisms listed above
- are accessible and user-friendly
- challenge Readers/Preachers to think for themselves
- use existing publications (book, DVD etc.) as its basis e.g.:
    - o   a theological resource
    - o   a devotional resource
    - o   a practical worship/preaching resource
    - o   a novel / current affairs/DVD resource(s)
- address through accompanying study guides:
    - o   spiritual development
    - o   the practicalities of leading worship and preaching
    - o   theological reflection
      as well as
    - o   knowledge and understanding from further study
      (whatever the main focus of the resource itself)
- would represent 2 hours per week over 9 months (i.e. between 6 and 12 months)

2   commission study guides funded ecumenically for publication on a web-site, to 'wrap around' the four existing and readily available publications (as above) specified each year that build a rolling collection of resources for continuing development thus:

- o 4 resources to choose from in year 1
- o 8 resources to choose from in year 2
- o 12 resources to choose from in year 3
- o then in year 4, the shelf-life of the first 4 would end as the next 4 were introduced. This way at the local level, the publication (book/DVD etc) could be shared from one preacher to another from one year to another.

3   **invite regional partnerships** to offer regional ecumenical events and library access related to some of the resource materials in the rolling collection

4   **publish an attractive, annual log-book/journal** which enables participants to reflect and record their development (which could contribute to evidence of development required by some denominations) and to give an annual point for completion and starting afresh (avoiding that never-ending distant-horizon feel that Continuing Development so easily has).

This strategy is cost-effective (and cheap!) to run and maintain. It is nationwide in concept, but has local and regional applications. It allows different emphases and focal points in different years. It enables a low-key start to pilot the venture. From the third year of operation it can offer a wide range of resources that could entice more people to take part.

Section 5

Ways forward

Change

To achieve the kind of training we envisage is going to involve change for everyone involved. At present the United Reformed Church and the Methodist Church both train their Preachers through national programmes, while the Church of England trains Readers through diocesan programmes. All these programmes have been (or are still being) changed and refined, each seeking to provide a more effective and efficient programme for those who are training to be Readers/Preachers. This is our common driving force for change. We recognize weaknesses in current provision, agree where improvements need to be made and then consider how best to improve effectiveness (including cost-effectiveness) and efficiency.

'A vision for good practice' is a key contribution to such discussion and agreement in regional partnerships. The nature and extent of change is in the hands of each regional partnership, as are the ways in which the transition is made from current provision to the new.

The following paragraphs aim to inform transition management by indicating how partner denominations are likely to view change to regional provision.

A view from the Church of England

A National Scheme to diocesan schemes

Until 1990 the Church of England provided a national programme. However, dioceses had increasingly devised their own schemes and abandoned the national one. In 1989 ACCM Occasional Paper 32, *The Training of Readers* required every dioceses to provide its own training scheme and brought in the present moderation system.

Moderation

Moderation was designed to ensure that diocesan schemes meet national criteria. It is supervised by the Ministry Division's Reader Education Panel and a national moderator. It operates through a system of regional groups. In the light of the move towards regional partnerships which will include various forms of training, there will be a review (due to start in November 2005) of the various schemes for moderation and inspection operating in our churches.

The current scene

The current scene is marked by considerable variety. In different parts of England there are:

- dioceses where Readers do their training entirely on their own;
- dioceses where Reader undertake training alongside other lay people, locally acknowledged lay ministers and ordinands;
- dioceses where Readers and OLMs train together, and a few where Readers, OLMs and other clergy train together;
- dioceses which collaborate with each other in the training of Readers, as of clergy;
- a diocese, an archdeaconry and a new town where Reader/Preacher training is delivered ecumenically;
- dioceses whose Reader training programmes are accredited with HE institutions;
- dioceses whose Reader training programmes are not accredited, including some that used to be.

Issues of concern

Equipping the Saints, the 2003 report on Reader Training, rejoiced in a continuing improvement of standards in Reader training nationally, but also noted the following issues of concern in diocesan programmes:

- It is possible for a diocese to introduce a new Reader training programme without any consultation to ensure that it meets the national criteria.
- Dioceses whose programmes have been accredited by HE institutions may have been accredited at level 1 or at level 2.
- Low numbers of Readers in training in some areas seriously affect the quality of training.
- In dioceses where there are other episcopally licensed lay ministers Reader training tends to be more narrowly focused, and as a result may not meet the national criteria.
- Many dioceses rely too heavily on one person for the oversight and delivery of training. Directors of Training often have additional and disparate responsibilities.

We would add to these:

- It is often difficult, especially when numbers are low, to meet the needs of the less academically able candidate at the same time as stretching those who are academically very able, possibly having a degree in theology.
- There is little consistency about the status of those who have been trained in a sister church. In some dioceses a Methodist or URC Preacher is warmly welcomed and given minimal training before admission as a Reader. In others such people are expected to do 3 years' training.
- Accreditation with an HE institution can be costly in terms of both money and time. This prevents some dioceses from seeking accreditation. Others are deterred by a sense that the HE institution wants to 'move the goal posts'.

A view from the United Reformed Church and the Methodist Church

Implementation of *Formation for Ministry within a Learning Church* only has an impact on the development of ecumenical training of Lay Preachers / Local Preachers in England. In Scotland and Wales, ecumenical developments are happening at different paces. As a result, the United Reformed Church and the Methodist Church will need to keep their existing national provision operating outside England for longer periods than inside England.

National training bodies in the two denominations will need to endorse the Training Specification. When this is done, they will need to:

- take part in ecumenical discussions about moderation and quality arrangements;
- take part in the initial approval of each regional partnership's programme;
- specify safeguards to ensure an orderly transition from national provision to regional provision;
- consider how and when each denomination can move from national provision to regional programmes without causing decreasing national cohorts and increasing overheads and staff resources;
- be part of an ecumenical moderation and review procedure to monitor each region's provision and to provide quality assurance of initial training for the two denominations.

Some examples from current collaborations

Readers and clergy

Faced in 1990 with the need to devise a new programme for training Readers one diocese chose to train them alongside ordinands on the local course – 'piggy-backing'. The first Moderation report, while full of praise for many excellent features, noted that the Reader candidates felt like second-class citizens, and there was little in the way of Reader formation. In a number of dioceses Readers now share part of their training with ordinands (most often candidates for OLM).

Two dioceses

When Readers from two dioceses train together it tends to be through using the same course. In one case the initial prompt came through the local HE institution. Diocesan officers discovered that the local course was in the process of submitting a new programme which included Readers. The two dioceses were already training clergy on the same course, so that training their Readers together was a natural development. Both dioceses brought their particular strengths to the partnership.

Ecumenical training

There are three areas where Readers/Preachers are already training together, ranging from a whole diocese to a large town. In two cases, two churches are involved in the training, but in the third, four churches are involved. The moderators had much praise for the programme which they looked at, and believed it could be a model for other areas. There has been no single reason for working ecumenically. It has been a response to a gospel imperative as well as a response to relatively small numbers.

HE institutions

There are many partnerships between diocese and HE institutions. Not all are equally happy. Those that work best are with institutions that regard the diocese as a true partner.

Lessons learned

Partnerships founder or are unhappy, when one party feels:

- their needs are not heard;
- their resources and strengths are not appreciated;
- like a second class citizen.

Partnerships succeed when each member:

- feels themselves to be a valued contributor;
- has a good understanding of their own resources, strengths and weaknesses;
- appreciates the resources and strengths of the other partners.

Section 6

Action for change

Partner churches finding a collaborative way forward

We recommend that partner churches amplify the learning outcomes implied in the training specification to indicate how Reader/Preacher training:

- is properly related to ordination training;
- is distinct from ordination training;
- has a sense of progression through initial training and through continuing development.

We recommend that partner churches set up a single ecumenical process for quality and accountability for Reader/Preacher training programmes.

Regional partnerships finding your own collaborative ways forward

1. Talk within your own diocese / denomination about your current provision, its strengths, weaknesses and how it is managed.

2. Listen to regional partners at all levels describe their provision in order to understand viewpoints, emphases, concerns and hopes.

3. Study and discuss the Training Specification.

4. Evaluate as partners the current forms of provision in the light of the Training Specification.

5. Consider how current forms of provision can contribute to a new regional programme that meets the Training Specification.

6. Establish a process for designing the new regional programme.

7. Ensure that proposed regional developments are acceptable to dioceses and denominations, and have been worked through with ministerial training and HE institutions.

8. Contribute to ecumenical negotiations about quality procedures.

9. Agree a process and a timescale for an orderly transition from existing forms of provision to the new regional programme.

10. Do it and review it!

A vision for good practice in Reader/Preacher training

The Reader Task Group does not under estimate the issues and concerns that regional partnerships face in developing Reader/Preacher training, but we hope that our own happy experience of:

- working together as a Task Group,
- building goodwill between partners,
- being honest with each other about our situations and concerns,
- sharing commitment to a common goal,
- finding practical and realistic ways forward,

makes it easier for your regional partnership to develop your own Reader/Preacher training programme.

Appendix

Membership

The Reader Task Group   was formed in January 2004;

held nine meetings during its 15-month life and one 24-hour residential by 3 of its members;

held one joint meeting with the Education for Discipleship Task Group;

received 25 responses on its proposals;

has been a positive and encouraging experience in diocesan and ecumenical partnership.

Mr Geoff Budd   (chair) Chair of Diocese of Wakefield Reader Training Steering Group and moderator of Reader training

Mrs Margaret Baxter   Chair of the Reader Education Panel, Ministry Division

Mrs Margaret Hounsham   Director of Reader Training, Portsmouth Diocese (member of the group until summer 2004)

Revd David Jenkins   United Reformed Church; until August 2004, Programme Co-ordinator, Training for Learning and Serving

Mr Peter Relf   Methodist Church, Connexional Secretary for Local Preachers

Dr David Way   Theological Education Secretary, Ministry Division

Revd Alec George   (secretary) National Moderator of Reader Training, Ministry Division

Part 3

Parameters of the curriculum

and

Post-ordination phase of IME

A report of the

implementation task groups

Section 1

Introduction

The two task groups on the curriculum and the post-ordination phase of training were set two primary tasks:

In the light of 'A statement of Ministerial Expectations for Ministerial Education' (*Formation for Ministry within a Learning Church,* hereafter 'the report of 2003', pp. 57–9) to draw up parameters for the curriculum for ordinands in the pre-ordination and post-ordination phases.

To work on guidance to dioceses and training institutions on good practice for the post-ordination phase of IME, including guidelines for training ministers and churches to explain the new approach to training.

Our report focuses on the education and training of ordained ministers and makes practical recommendations to shape curriculum and training relationships. This is therefore an exercise in practical theology which embodies and discloses beliefs about the nature of ministry, the nature of Church and the mission of God in the world.

The Church exists for mission as does a fire for burning

The recommendations of 2003, we believe, are a direct and immediate contribution to the missionary character of the whole Church. Its vision in relation to ordained ministries is to 'provide high quality training for the clergy that will equip them to offer vibrant and collaborative spiritual leadership, to empower a vocationally motivated laity and, thereby, to promote and serve God's mission in the world' (para 1.3).

The Church as the body of Christ

The report identified in the educational processes and institutional relationships that currently serve ministerial formation a number of critical fractures, and as a result sought a more holistic vision. Partnership, collaboration, and integration are key terms which flow from a vision of the Church as the Body of Christ in which the limbs are bound together, not by proximity or convenience, but by the ligaments and sinews of consciously chosen collaboration within the economy of the Holy Spirit. Reconfiguring relationships between dioceses/districts/synods and theological institutions is not simply a pragmatic proposal, but an outworking of our essential interdependence in the Body of Christ. It invites a radical shift in our understanding from seeing churches and dioceses as purchasers from training institutions and rather seeing them as partners.

The Church as participation in the life of God

Collaboration between established structures and institutional cultures can be demanding and time consuming. It involves making new relationships, learning new languages, letting go of existing ways of working and developing the skills, deep knowledge and character that we seek to encourage in the Church at large. It involves re-imagining the world we inhabit. A vision of the kingdom of God calls Christian disciples to a continual process of transformation and renewal not only at the personal level, but in social and institutional ways of relating. The tasks of implementing this report offer to regional partners in each place not only a means towards the end of a more effective, mission-shaped Church, but an opportunity to work out in each particular context, the consequences of the outpouring of the Spirit at Pentecost.

Ministry as radical discipleship

The report of 2003 emphasizes the commitment of the whole people of God to lifelong discipleship of Jesus Christ which involves personal and spiritual development, learning and reflection. The parameters for the curriculum set out in this report offer a framework within which ordained ministers may develop their particular obedience as disciples called to leadership within the churches. We stress, therefore, the continuity of this calling with Christian discipleship, the continuity of education and training 'before' and 'after' ordination, the integration of learning that is both experiential, academically critical and reflective. For trainee ministers throughout Initial Ministerial Education (IME), from entry in this process to the point at which the ordained minister has completed a supervised first appointment, the proposal is that the study, learning, practice and supervision are integral to ministerial life.

This approach is grounded in an understanding of theology as *habitus* which lays the stress not upon the acquisition of knowledge or skills, but upon the development of people of faith within communities that shape Christian living. At all stages of the formational process the report of 2003 envisages that character (being/spirituality/vocation) is being transformed in Christ through engagement with self, others, Scripture and the Christian tradition (doing/skills/practice) for the sake of deep knowledge (metanoia/practical wisdom).

Thus, the vision of the report of 2003 is that the resources of the theological institutions will be available to those in training, through regional training partnerships, not only in the first years of IME, but also in the latter years when the focus has shifted to a parish, church or circuit. Likewise, the practical wisdom of local contexts and local supervisors will be available to inform the design and delivery of syllabuses through the participation in the training partnership of those responsible for supervising the early years of ministry.

The Church as formative faith community

In addition, at each stage, the communities in which patterns of Christian living are being shaped are key to the development of the student minister. The report of 2003 invites more careful and systematic attention to the roles of different formational communities throughout IME, and how the supervised ministerial settings of the later phase is an explicit dimension of this. A Church of England training parish and training incumbent, a URC minister's internship context and a Methodist Probationer's first circuit, are not identical, but the principle holds good that first ministerial appointments are key in formation. We anticipate that the contribution to the learning process of those involved in practical supervision in the local context will be enhanced in two ways. First, by a greater clarity about roles: what the relative roles of supervising ministers, mentors, academic tutors and those in oversight are for each denomination; second, by the provision of training which will enable parishes, churches and circuits to be intentional and reflective about the ethos in which students and newly appointed ministers are being formed as well as becoming more skilled in the formal supervision of those beginning public ministry.

Such an emphasis on the formation of *habitus* in Christian communities takes seriously the historical and corporate nature of the Church in which faith is nurtured in continuity with a great cloud of witnesses. It also lays the emphasis in theological study upon the nurturing of human beings who know God to be the ground and source of their being, are confident and fluent enough in the Scriptures and Christian tradition as a lived reality that they can be open to others whose experience is different. In this way they will be able to help the entire people of God to bear courageous and generous witness to the riches God offers in Jesus Christ.

Shared vision: different pathways to a common *telos*

It is envisaged that when the report of 2003 is implemented, Initial Ministerial Education will constitute a continuous and coherent personal and ministerial development process. This has the potential to improve significantly not only the quality of theological education and ministerial formation that is offered, but also the quality of experience for all those who are engaged in it – training institutions, diocesan/district/synod training officers, and the candidates/ministers themselves. Many who work in this area know the frustrations that come from a fragmented and incoherent provision, in which we struggle to build on or hand over to others in anything approaching an adequate way; many know the pressures and difficulties that come from attempting to do everything in very small institutions; there is enough concern from churches, candidates and training institutions to cast doubt on whether the process as we have it gives confidence that our ministers are 'fit to practice', and such doubt saps energy.

In four areas these recommendations require a coherent and continuous approach:

1. Between a variety of institutions, officers and local ministry contexts and supervisors who will contribute to the formation of each potential minister in each newly formed regional training partnership.
2. Between regional training partnerships so that potential ministers who move region during their training can expect to build on prior learning rather than repeat what they have already done.
3. Between the three denominations who are signatories to this report and other churches as appropriate in the various regional partnerships and settings for ministry.
4. In understanding the potential minister as a person, who, throughout the formational process needs to be nurtured within community as a person of character, skills and knowledge.

However, although a high degree of collaboration is needed the model of engagement between different parties and different phases and modes of education is not one of homogenization. There will remain a variety of routes through training, depending on previous experience, education and personal circumstances. The parameters for the curriculum are intended to be a framework which allows for creativity, innovation and contextual syllabus design. Although a shared vision has emerged between the Church of England, The United Reformed Church and the Methodist Church about the learning outcomes which will shape the kind of ordained ministers which the churches in England need today, there remain profoundly different ways of being church and significantly different dynamics in formation for ministry which cannot be easily collapsed into one another. This has significantly shaped the structure of this report with the need for specific appendices that complement the report for our different denominations.

So the recommendations of 2003 enable the reconfiguring of initial ministerial education not primarily around a pre-determined timetable for ordination followed by readiness for wider responsibility but in relation to the variable time by which a person may be deemed ready for ordination or for wider responsibility. This means that many practices and assumptions that currently shape pre- and post-ordination training are open to revision. In pre-ordination training the assumption that preparation for ordination is determined by a fixed number of years yields to a serious and careful attention to what this candidate needs for fitness to minister as a public representative of the Church's life and faith. These judgements are complex, for they require discernment about how prior learning and experience is in this person formative of an ordained ministry and life. Shaping a training pathway is complex, for individual learning needs have to be balanced with the creation of stable cohorts/communities of faith which are essential for ministerial and personal development.

We are very aware of the challenges that have been present even in our narrow remit. We offer this report as a contribution to an ongoing dialogue with the churches and training institutions and training officers. Because IME has operated in two domains, pre- and post-ordination, different cultures and assumptions are also operative. Pre-ordination provision is used to thinking in terms of validation, quality control mechanisms from the churches and HE bodies; they almost universally operate within frameworks of curriculum content, modular programmes, specified aims and objectives, formal assessment, and tightly structured reporting; institutions that deliver this training are frequently ecumenical, and the churches' procedures for quality control are always ecumenical. Some post-ordination provision shares some of these features, but much does not. An integrated curriculum and process of delivery carries with it some major changes of culture for all parties, but communicating these, and in particular communicating them to such diverse groups at the same time, is by no means easy.

Finally, the challenges have been evident as we have explored more carefully the practices of the partner churches. There are analogies, parallels and shared issues, but there is no direct equivalence between curates, probationers, and interns; there are significant differences in timescales between the training needs of Anglican, Methodist and URC ministers, and there are significant differences in the roles of supervising ministers. These are not simply accidental differences; they reflect our different understandings of ordained ministry, our different polities, as well as our different resources. The implications for a reconfigured IME are different for each partner church. Methodist members of the task groups endorse the main report and raise issues and questions for further consideration by the Methodist Church in Appendix 1. The United Reformed Church members endorse the main report but in the context of their own church's training review recommend that the issues and questions identified are fed into that process.

The process of producing this report

This report is itself the joint product of two task groups, the first focusing on the parameters of the curriculum in the pre- and post-ordination phases of the new IME and the second on the particular issues of the post-ordination phase, often referred to as CME 1–4. The two groups worked initially to investigate their own areas and then in the second period they worked together to produce this single report. This process and the ecumenical nature of the two groups were in themselves a stimulating and, we trust, productive process. The names of the members of the two groups are set out in Appendix 7.

The two draft reports were also sent out for consultation in December 2004. Many individual issues were raised but the main themes of the consultation were as follows:

1   Nearly 80 per cent of responses were generally affirmative of the direction and tenor of the draft reports.

2   Some commented that the work was overly focused on the needs of future stipendiary parochial clergy. We have sought to redress this and to address the full range of ordained clergy, both full-time and various types of part-time.

3   There was strong backing for a Learning Outcomes type approach to the curriculum and a few voices who called for something more like a core curriculum or an indication of actual content. We believe that our churches have good experience of working with broad learning outcomes and that we should continue with this approach, while noting that the new Learning Outcomes are much more detailed than their predecessors.

4   We have strengthened the Learning Outcomes in the areas of ministerial and spiritual formation, communication and mission and in the specific area of engaging with other faiths, in response to the comments of the House of Bishops and other correspondents.

5   A few correspondents raised the question of whether the time identified for learning in the post-ordination phase was too demanding for NSMs or indeed for stipendiary ministers. Some thought that trying to express this goal in 'days' was not the most helpful way. We have revisited this issue trying to strike a balance between the fundamental points made in the original report (continuing learning is a part of ministry; reconfiguring IME to include

a post-ordination phase; establishing patterns of lifelong learning) and a practical and properly flexible guideline.

6   A few raised issues which were beyond our terms of reference and for which detailed proposals have not yet been developed, e.g. what form of quality and accountability framework should be drawn up for the new IME. We have pointed here to the work that has yet to be done.

We are grateful to all who corresponded with us and we have sought to build on the best insights of the contributions made to us.

Section 2

Learning outcomes for ordained ministry

Requirements for IME and suitability for further responsibility

Formation for Ministry within a Learning Church begins its statement of expectation for ministerial education with a summary statement as follows:

The Church seeks that all God's people grow in faith, deepen their discipleship, and learn more deeply to 'inhabit godly wisdom'. As part of God's people, and in order to enable such growth in others, the Church seeks ministers who:

- *Are firmly rooted in their love of God, discipleship of Jesus Christ, and dedicated to a deepening pilgrimage of faith in the Holy Spirit;*

- *Are passionate about the transformation of the whole created order into one that reflects the redemptive love of God;*

- *Are deeply committed to loving service in the Church as sign and instrument of God's love for the world;*

- *Immerse themselves, with faithful obedience, in the Church's life of prayer and worship, and its critical engagement with Scripture and the Christian tradition;*

- *Are dedicated to bringing their gifts of leadership, pastoral care, worship and mission to the service of the Church through their calling to ordination.* (p. 57)

This statement concentrates not on curriculum content, but on the character and personal qualities of those who will serve the Church in ordained ministry. In this it echoes *Ministry and Mission* and its primary aim for theological education:

to enable the student to grow in those personal qualities by which, with and through the corporate ministry of the Church, the creative and redemptive activity of God may be proclaimed and realised in the world. (*Mission and Ministry*, p. 23)

The report of 2003 therefore builds on the work of *Mission and Ministry* in recommending that the heart of theological education is not coverage of a set of subjects or achievement of particular qualifications, but the development of character within the context of the Church's life.

Our aim in developing our proposals has been to do the following:

To give priority to the key aim of reconfiguring initial training as the whole period of training, before and after ordination, up to the point of transition either to a post of responsibility or to a recognized moment of completion of IME in a post of continuing assistant ministry. In this report the phrase IME is used to refer to this re-configured pattern, differentiating the two phases of pre- and post-ordination training where necessary.

To offer parameters and guidance to enable trainers within regional partnerships to design pathways and curricula that give continuity and coherence of training in this initial phase.

To highlight various key issues for those within regions as they work on curriculum design and the steps that will be necessary to implement them within a region.

To provide stimulus to trainers to think in fresh ways about key dimensions of the training process – for example, with regard to assessment or the shape of the training relationship in the post-ordination phase.

In each of these areas we offer guidance and stimulus rather than prescription. We have found in our own discussions rich seams to mine which will be replicated in regional partnerships as they do their work, and we wish to share some of the fruits of this discussion. We have not defined more precisely curriculum content or a syllabus, and we are aware that those who have urged us to do this will be disappointed; but we are convinced that the method adopted by the report of 2003 was correct and that agreed parameters for the curriculum can enable two things:

to provide the framework within which detailed curriculum development can take place, sensitive to the resources, contexts and priorities of each partnership;

to provide the framework within which dialogue can take place between regions.

Our key objectives have been that the new IME will:

Be flexible so as to build on prior learning (earlier studies or ministerial experience; Education for Discipleship; training for another authorized ministry etc.);

Give continuity of learning in the pre- and post-ordination phases;

Identify clearly qualities and skills required for posts of responsibility;

Enable coherent planning of a candidate's pathway from discernment of vocation through training and towards the post of responsibility or a second phase of ministry beyond IME;

Equip candidates/clergy better in terms of their theological and ministerial preparation;

Provide opportunity for many to work at degree level and beyond by the time of completion of IME;

Reduce the pressure on the pre-ordination curriculum;

Work within a candidate-focused approach where training is no longer determined by the current Bishops' Regulations but according to the Church's needs and the candidate's potential and needs, within an overall budget for training agreed each year by Synod.

Introduction to the Learning Outcomes

The Learning Outcomes are central to our report and have been formally approved by the Church of England's House of Bishops. They develop the framework offered in the report of 2003 by taking seriously the criticisms that were directed to those statements. Since there is considerable scope for misunderstanding what Learning Outcomes are, and how they might be used, we wish to signal as clearly as possible the following points:

1   The statements are designed to provide widely agreed expectations of the qualities, understanding and skills the Church requires of those being ordained, and the development of those qualities, understanding and skills that the Church requires for those moving to a position of responsibility. For those continuing in an assistant ministry they indicate the direction and domains for continued learning and development. They are designed to be sufficiently focused and brief to give guidance to trainers as they take on the challenging task of designing new curricula, but sufficiently open to enable creative approaches in terms of methods and content.

2   The Learning Outcomes in the main body of the text are related to and organized within the framework provided by the selection criteria of the Church of England to give one set of outcomes expected at the point of ordination, another at the point of completion of IME, and additional outcomes for fitness to take a post of responsibility. The strength of this approach is that it starts from an already widely recognized and valued set of criteria, and makes explicit the way in which IME develops and builds on these. The Methodist Church believes that there are two possible ways of drawing up the Learning Outcomes in relation to the selection categories of the Methodist Church. We set these out in Appendix 1. While not having formal selection categories of its own, the United Reformed Church believes that it can relate these Learning Outcomes to its own procedures.

3   The statements offer outcomes for key moments within IME – the point of ordination and the completion of IME. By providing outcomes for each point we indicate elements of progression between pre- and post-ordination training. Sometimes this is expressed in terms of the depth of engagement, sometimes in terms of the range of opportunities or contexts that are available at different phases in the process.

4   We have delineated Learning Outcomes for 'a post of responsibility' which is a further stage for some, but by no means all, candidates. The most obvious, but not only, category to which it refers is the priest exercising sole responsibility. It is not necessarily expected that a person holding 'a post of responsibility' will be stipendiary.

5   We have not used HE level descriptors as a template for these statements, mindful of the caution about using such levels in a prescriptive way, and the concern that they can skew the learning process in particular directions. However, Level 2 – Diploma – has been agreed as a normal expectation at the point of ordination, and therefore at this point the statements of the qualities, understanding and skills sought reflect and echo HE level 2 descriptors, since they express what is expected for those learning and practising within defined parameters and under supervision. The qualities, understanding and skills at the point of completion of IME are expressed in terms that echo HE Level 3 descriptors, since they express what is expected for those learning and practising within broad parameters, with little supervision, and where creativity and integration are required. Curriculum designers need to attend to how accreditation at HE levels operates within these parameters, but we are not suggesting that a particular outcome has to be assessed at a particular HE Level.

6   Some have urged that we prescribe how the length of training, or the content of training is to be determined. To do this would require us either to offer a core curriculum, or to define precise benchmarks for each phase. This was neither in our task description, nor does it seem to us desirable, as responses to the consultation has overwhelmingly confirmed. Instead, we believe that careful thought has to be given about the structures and relationships between those responsible for training to make these decisions in a collaborative, consultative manner.

7   In order to reduce the front-loading of education and training in the pre-ordination period the Learning Outcomes recognize that selection has to be made about what can and should be done. Here we endorse the comments of *Mission and Ministry*, and many prior reports, that speak of relativizing the claims of any discipline, subject, or skill to the overall aims, and to resist the pressure to 'cover' or do everything. Being realistic about selection is, in our view, an opportunity to be more intentional and focused, and to be clear for all concerned about the rationale for what is being done and what is not. Curriculum design needs to provide a clear rationale for the selection of settings, and how these can be most effectively used at different stages in training. One of the most important factors in the re-configuring of initial training to encompass the pre- and post- ordination phases is to

develop trust that the learning and opportunities can and will be coherent and progressive across the phases. It is therefore crucial that within regional partnerships there is genuine collaboration and partnership between the personnel currently closely identified with each phase so that this trust and understanding can develop.

8   The Learning Outcomes inevitably focus on the individual concerned. However, this should not be read as endorsing an individualized learning programme. We do not believe that there should be, or will need to be, debate about the need to learn, practice and experience formation with, alongside and through others. Nor do we think that anyone will seriously argue that a student never learns as an individual or independently. What needs to be developed are clear rationale for how and why groups are gathered, and how they enable different kinds of learning, practice, reflection and formation. Such a rationale needs to include factors around immersion and separation, continuity of groups and collusion within groups, homogeneity and heterogeneity within groups, stability and change.

Learning Outcomes for IME

The Learning Outcomes are an important element within the report, but they should not be read in isolation. They are set within:

*   the Church's foundation in and orientation to mission, to ministry as radical discipleship rooted in Christian communities which form, shape and sustain such discipleship and ministry;

*   the understanding that Initial Ministerial Education, in both its pre- and post-ordination phases, is a rich process of formation that weaves knowing, being and doing, or understanding, character and practice.

The Learning Outcomes have a particular and focused purpose. They provide a framework or parameters within which curricula can be designed. They set out succinctly and clearly what is expected or required of ordinands and the newly ordained (and of those who may move to a post of responsibility), to ensure that there is agreement about the goals or outcomes at any phase. Learning Outcomes cannot say everything, for this risks a 'tick box' mentality, but they are designed to say enough to give guidance to those who are responsible for shaping the process and content of IME. Even though the term 'curriculum' is understood broadly as a means of enabling the formation of the person, the curriculum is not the sole means of enabling formation, and therefore these Learning Outcomes are not exhaustive descriptions or statements of all that happens in the process by which a person is formed in and for ordained ministry. Thus, for example, candidates' growth in a life of prayer, godliness and the personal qualities required for ministry will continue to be the subject of reporting to bishops by principals.

The Learning Outcomes have been revised to take account of the advice and comment of the House of Bishops, especially in strengthening the sections in spirituality and worship.

Learning outcome statements for ordained ministry within the Church of England

At selection candidates should	At the point of ordination candidates should	At completion of IME candidates should	In addition, in order to be licensed to a post of incumbent status or equivalent responsibility candidates should
Vocation Be able to speak to their sense of vocation to ministry and mission, referring both to their own conviction and to the extent to which others have confirmed it. Their sense of vocation should be obedient, realistic and informed.	Be able to give an account of their vocation to ministry and mission and their readiness to receive and exercise ordained ministry as a deacon within the Church of God.	Be able to give an account of their vocation to ministry and mission and their readiness to receive and exercise ordained ministry as a priest within the Church of God.	Demonstrate capacity to bear a public and representative role in ministry and mission, and a readiness to exercise oversight and leadership in their ordained ministry.
	Demonstrate proficiency in a range of skills and abilities needed to exercise public ministry under supervision by being able to show basic skills as a reflective practitioner.	Demonstrate proficiency in a broad range of skills and abilities needed to exercise public ministry and leadership of a local church, and the ability to do this in relatively unsupervised settings. Show developed skills as an effective reflective practitioner.	Demonstrate proficiency in the skills needed to exercise leadership and supervision of others in a position of responsibility by being able to show sophisticated skills as an effective reflective practitioner and the capacity to develop these further.
Ministry within the Church of England Be familiar with the tradition and practice of the Church of England and be ready to work within them.	Demonstrate familiarity with the legal (including the Act of Synod), canonical and administrative responsibilities appropriate to the newly ordained and those working under supervision.	Demonstrate working understanding of and good practice in the legal, canonical and administrative responsibilities of those in public ministry with supervised responsibilities.	Demonstrate working understanding of and good practice in the legal, canonical and administrative responsibilities of those having oversight and responsibility.
	Be rooted in corporate worship in the traditions and practices of the Church of England, showing gifts and ability in leading public worship and preaching in ways that show understanding of and good practice in liturgy and worship.	Demonstrate gifts for and proficiency in leading public worship and preaching, showing understanding of and good practice in liturgy and worship in a wide range of settings.	Demonstrate skill in presiding in public worship in the congregation(s) in ways that foster rich corporate worship.
	Demonstrate awareness of the church's roles and opportunities in public life and institutions, and in relation to secular agencies and other faith communities.	Demonstrate working understanding of the practices of Christian ministry in a range of public settings, agencies and faith communities.	Demonstrate ability to take a leading role in working with other partners, representing the Church in public life and other institutions, and working with other faith leaders where possible.
	Show understanding of the insights and practices of other churches and traditions in worship, especially of ecumenical partners.	Demonstrate engagement with ecumenical working relationships, especially with covenanting partners.	Demonstrate the ability to work ecumenically and to encourage ecumenical co-operation.

At selection candidates should	At the point of ordination candidates should	At completion of IME candidates should	In addition, in order to be licensed to a post of incumbent status or equivalent responsibility candidates should
Spirituality Show evidence of a commitment to a spiritual discipline, involving individual and corporate prayer and worship. Their spiritual practice should be such as to sustain and energize them in their daily lives.	Demonstrate commitment to loving service in the Church rooted in a sustained and growing love of God, discipleship of Christ, and pilgrimage in faith in the Holy Spirit.	Demonstrate loving service in the Church, expressed in effective and collaborative leadership, discipleship of Christ, and continued pilgrimage in faith in the Holy Spirit.	Demonstrate loving service in the Church, in personal discipleship, in diaconal and priestly ministry, in collaborative leadership and oversight of others, and in faithful response to the leading of the Holy Spirit.
	Show evidence of a life increasingly formed and sustained by trust in and dependence on the gifting and grace of God.	Show evidence of a life and ministry formed, sustained and energised by trust in and dependence on the gifting and grace of God.	
	Be rooted and growing in a life of prayer shaped faithfully within the demands and disciplines of initial training and the expectations of public ministry.	Be rooted and growing in a life of prayer shaped faithfully within the expectations of public ministry, corporate and personal worship and devotion.	Form and sustain a life of prayer that provides sustenance for the strains and joys of leadership.
Personality and character Candidates should be sufficiently mature and stable to show that they are able to sustain the demanding role of a minister and to face change and pressure in a flexible and balanced way. They should be seen to be people of integrity.	Show insight, openness, maturity, integrity and stability in the face of pressure and changing circumstances.	Show insight, openness, maturity, integrity and stability in the pressure and change entailed in public ministry.	Be able to facilitate and enable change.
	Reflect with insight on personal strengths and weaknesses, the gifts brought and vulnerability; and demonstrate appropriate development.	Reflect with insight on personal strengths and weaknesses, the gifts brought and vulnerability in response to a new context of public ministry.	Engage with others to reflect with insight on a personal style of leadership, its strengths and weaknesses in context, and demonstrate appropriate development.
	Exercise appropriate care of self, using the support provided in initial training.	Exercise appropriate care of self, through developing sustainable patterns of life and work, and effective support networks in the context of public ministry.	Exercise appropriate care of self, through developing sustainable patterns of life and work, and effective support networks and facilitate the appropriate care of colleagues.

At selection candidates should	At the point of ordination candidates should	At completion of IME candidates should	In addition, in order to be licensed to a post of incumbent status or equivalent responsibility candidates should
Relationships Candidates should demonstrate self-awareness and self-acceptance as a basis for developing open and healthy professional, personal and pastoral relationships as ministers. They should respect the will of the Church on matters of sexual morality.	Form and sustain relationships, both with those who are like-minded and those who differ, marked by integrity, empathy, respect, honesty and insight.	Form and sustain relationships across a wide range of people, including in situations of conflict and disagreement, marked by integrity, empathy, respect, honesty and insight.	Show skill and sensitivity in resolving issues of conflict within the church community and the formation of a corporate life in the presence of diversity within that community.
	Demonstrate good practice in a limited range of pastoral relationships, and learn from these experiences.	Demonstrate good practice in a wide range of pastoral and professional relationships.	Demonstrate the ability to supervise others in the conduct of pastoral relationships.
Leadership and collaboration Candidates should show ability to offer leadership in the Church community and to some extent in the wider community. This ability includes the capacity to offer an example of faith and discipleship, to collaborate effectively with others, as well as to guide and shape the life of the church community in its mission to the world.	Demonstrate openness toward and ability to gain from experiences and practices of being supervised.	Demonstrate ability to supervise others in a limited range of roles and responsibilities.	Demonstrate ability to supervise and manage others, both lay and ordained in formal settings of training and practice.
	Demonstrate effective collaborative leadership and an ability to work in teams in a limited range of settings, and learn from these experiences.	Exercise effective collaborative leadership, working effectively as a member of team, as an ordained person.	Demonstrate effective collaborative leadership and the ability to exercise this in a position of responsibility.
	Demonstrate understanding of group dynamics especially in the settings of training, including the use and abuse of power.	Demonstrate ability to use understanding of group dynamics to participate in and lead groups and to reflect with insight on the use and abuse of power.	Show an integration and integrity of authority and obedience, leadership and service that enables the exercise of collaborative leadership.
	Exercise appropriate accountability and responsibility in faithfully and loyally receiving the authority of others in the context of training.	Exercise appropriate accountability and responsibility in a new ministerial context.	Exercise appropriate accountability and responsibility in faithfully and loyally receiving the authority of others, consistent with a position of responsibility.
	Exercise authority within the settings of the early years of formation and education that enables and empowers others in both personal and corporate lives.	Demonstrate appropriate use of authority in ways which enable and empower others in their mission and ministry, including colleagues.	Show an integration and integrity of authority and obedience, leadership and service that empowers and enables others in their leadership and service.

At selection candidates should	At the point of ordination candidates should	At completion of IME candidates should	In addition, in order to be licensed to a post of incumbent status or equivalent responsibility candidates should
Mission and evangelism Demonstrate a passion for mission that is reflected in thought, prayer and action. Understand the strategic issues and opportunities within the contemporary culture. Enable others to develop their vocations as witnesses and advocates of the good news.	Participate in and reflect on the mission of God in a selected range of social, ethical, cultural, religious and intellectual contexts in which Christian witness is to be lived out in acts of mercy, service and justice.	Participate in and reflect on the mission of God, identifying and engaging in issues of mission and social justice in the context of ministry.	Demonstrate understanding of the imperatives of the gospel and the nature of contemporary society and skills in articulating and engaging in appropriate forms of mission in response to them.
	Engage in and reflect upon practices of mission and evangelism, changing forms of church, and their relation to contexts, cultures, religions and contemporary spiritualities.	Demonstrate engagement in mission and evangelism in a range of contexts, particularly in the local community and in relation to the local church.	Demonstrate an ability to lead and enable others in faithful witness and to foster mission shaped churches.
	Show understanding of how children and adults learn, and how this is contributing to an ability to nurture others in their faith development.	Demonstrate an ability to nurture others in their faith development.	
	Communicate the gospel in a variety of media demonstrating sensitivity to audience and context.	Demonstrate ability to communicate gospel truth effectively in the context of ministry with different groups in church and community.	Enable others to articulate gospel truths and participate in their proclamation.

At selection candidates should	At the point of ordination candidates should	At completion of IME candidates should	In addition, in order to be licensed to a post of incumbent status or equivalent responsibility candidates should
Faith Candidates should show an understanding of the Christian faith and a desire to deepen their understanding. They should demonstrate personal commitment to Christ and a capacity to communicate the gospel.	Demonstrate a growing critical engagement with Scripture and the traditions of Christian thought, characterized by faithful obedience and openness to new insights.	Be able to engage confidently with the Bible as text and as Holy Scripture, as skilled interpreters and communicators in relation to fundamental traditions of Christian thought.	Demonstrate a readiness and openness for a ministry of oversight and vision, expressed in continued study, reflection, openness to new insights, maturity and physical self care.
	Form a life of study and reflection within the demands and disciplines of initial training and the expectations shaped by public ministry.	Form and sustain a life of disciplined study and reflection that sustains in public ministry.	Form and sustain a life of disciplined study and reflection that sustains in leadership.
Quality of mind Candidates should have the necessary intellectual capacity and quality of mind to undertake satisfactorily a course of theological study and ministerial preparation and to cope with the intellectual demands of ministry.	Show how personal commitment to Christ and discipleship is changing in the process of study and formation for ordained ministry.	Give an account of how personal commitment to Christ and discipleship is being shaped within the roles and expectations of ordained and public ministry.	Give an account of how personal commitment to Christ is being shaped within the roles and expectations of leadership and oversight of others.
	Interpret and use Scripture within limited contexts, showing a secure grasp of exegetical and hermeneutic skills, communicating this in various settings clearly, accurately, critically and openly.	Interpret and use Scripture across a wide range of settings, showing developed exegetical and hermeneutical skills, communicating an understanding and engagement with Scripture in ways that enable others to learn and explore.	
	Demonstrate understanding of the ways in which Christian beliefs and practices have developed in varying historical and cultural contexts.	Demonstrate continued and disciplined engagement with Christian beliefs and practices.	
	Demonstrate skill as reflective practitioners, able to engage thoughtfully and critically across the spectrum of Christian tradition, in ways that deeply inform personal practices, and which enable others to learn and explore.	Be skilled reflective practitioners, able to exercise wise and discerning judgement.	As skilled reflective practitioners demonstrate ability to energize and enable creative theologically informed practice.
	Demonstrate growing awareness of and reflective engagement with beliefs, practices and spiritualities of other faith traditions.		Demonstrate ability to develop and sustain dialogue with representatives of other religious traditions.

Section 3

Shaping the curriculum

Introduction

The Learning Outcomes provide parameters within which creative curriculum design can be developed. For this to happen in practice each region will need to set up a curriculum planning/programme design, which will bring together representatives of the different partners and institutions.

Programme designers will need to address a range of questions as they work with the learning outcomes, including:

- How should the Learning Outcomes shape the educational programmes?

- What are the kinds of learning that will take place within the programmes and what should be the balance between different elements of the curriculum?

- What style (or styles) of curriculum will be most appropriate to help students meet the learning outcomes?

- What is meant by 'integration', and where do different kinds of integration take place within programme as a whole?

- What are the appropriate forms of assessment, and how much of the programme will receive accreditation at diploma and degree level?

- What standard pathways through the programme are envisaged, and how will it be possible for students to transfer between regions at critical stages of the programme?

The Learning Outcomes and the educational programmes

The Learning Outcomes are expressed in broad domains and fields, rather than in terms of curriculum content or delivery. We are aware that there is vigorous debate among theological educators as to the best ways of designing a learning process in which the type of complex integration sought within the understanding, spirituality, personal qualities and skills of candidates and ministers can take place. We believe that regions should take responsibility for thinking through these issues and for stating the rationale for the choices they make – choices which will be influenced by context, resources, theological and institutional traditions etc. In this way, our work is in direct continuity with *Mission and Ministry* and its insistence that curricula are shaped within parameters and objectives that provide the criteria for the selection of what is learned and how it is delivered. The Learning Outcomes develop further the agreed expectations of *Mission and Ministry* in ways that we believe are more useful for curriculum design and that make explicit the continuity and progression in the pre- and post-ordination phases. We therefore restate some of the radical implications of *Mission and Ministry* for curriculum design:

1   all parts of the educational programme are to be seen in relation to, or relativized by, the central aim of theological education;

2   the divisions between the educational programme, between subjects, and between academic and practical, are also to be relativized by this central aim, and are of little or no importance in themselves;

3   the inclusion of any subject matter and method must be justified by its contribution to the objectives of the programme as whole.

Modes of learning and balance within the curriculum

As noted above, we have resisted the temptation to specify the content and style of learning at each stage of the process. This at least in part because we trust that training institutions/regions already have a good deal of expertise, and that as with the current validation process, it is likely that as programmes are developed so consensus will emerge. To help in this process we offer two models to provide stimulus for further thought.

A   For a programme to deliver the learning outcomes effectively it will need to enable the following kinds of learning at every stage:

1   Development of self-understanding and growing into the role: personal, affective learning;

2   Development of generic skills: critical thinking, self-awareness, collaborative working, etc.;

3   Disciplinary learning: sustained attention to biblical studies, doctrine, ethics, psychology, etc.;

4   Performance practice: writing and presenting, leading worship, preaching, pastoral conversation, group work (initially in class and on placement, later within ministerial practice);

5   Contextual learning/theological reflection on practice: sustained opportunities to make connections between practice and the theological and other disciplines.

All five of these elements will need to characterise both the pre- and the post-ordination phases, with integration a significant aim at every stage. We note that this permits, even encourages, flexibility of emphasis among the different types of learning, but not their separation. One way of expressing this in curriculum design is to be clear about the balance of time and weight given to these different types of learning at various phases of IME. Conceptually this may appear as follows:

| Affective learning: development of self-understanding etc. |
| Generic skills: critical thinking, collaborative working, leadership etc. |
| Disciplinary learning |
| Performance practice |
| Contextual learning |

Some of this weighting and time commitment will be expressed in terms of credits of modules, but not all learning and experience will be accredited in this way. Curricula that are discipline led need to attend to other dimensions of learning that can often be less visible, and appear less valued as a result. The opposite difficulty is present for thematic curricula, where attention to disciplines, and the learning that is required for integration to be effective, can often be less visible, and therefore appear less valued.

B One possible disadvantage of working with a set of Learning Outcomes rather than a core syllabus is that it is difficult to give a sense of the relative importance of different outcomes, and the impact this might have on curriculum design. For example, in our proposed 30 different outcomes, only two explicitly mention the study of Scripture. We do not intend by this to signal that the study of Scripture should occupy only 1/15 of a course of study.

Can we be more specific about the balance of content at different stages? The experience of validation over the past few years has been that there is a significant degree of convergence amongst pre-ordination programmes about the general balance of time and attention to be given to different areas of the curriculum. One way of approaching this from a 'disciplinary' approach would be to relate the Learning Outcomes to the following three broad streams of curriculum content:

Parameters of the curriculum and Post-ordination phase of IME

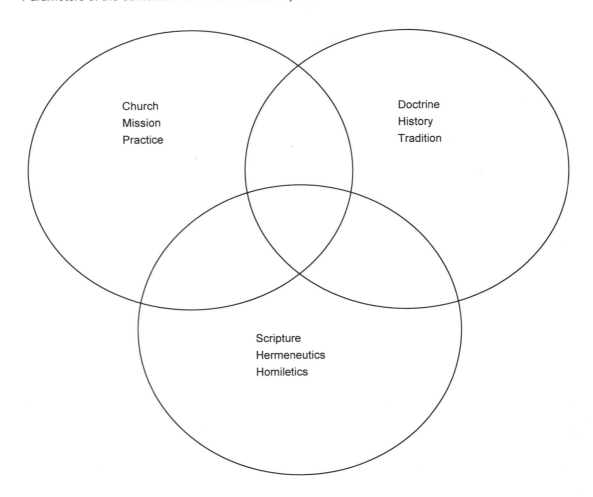

Church
Mission
Practice

Doctrine
History
Tradition

Scripture
Hermeneutics
Homiletics

Again, experience would suggest that these three streams have been given roughly equivalent weight, at least in terms of student time, if not always in terms of validated modules. A guideline for the distribution of study and learning might be that, in the pre-ordination phase, out of 240 credits at least 60 ought to belong in each group. This is not to say that these credits are attached to discrete modules, but that they provide guidance to the overall attention that is given to a curriculum stream within the overall programme. In the post-ordination phase, out of 120 credits at least 30 should belong to each group, with the expectation that the preponderance of the remaining 60 will be practice based.

This way of working with 'broad streams' of curriculum content is easiest to do when working with styles of curriculum that tend to discipline led models (see below). However, within more thematic and integrative approaches, as well as new patterns of mixed mode training, it is important that curriculum designers show how within modules balance of learning is achieved, and between modules how an overall balance of engagement is accomplished and assessed.

Styles of curriculum

The discussion above raises one of the most important questions that will face curriculum designers: what will be the basic orientation of the programme as a whole, and what will be the relationships between traditional theological disciplines, broad themes, etc.?

Some obvious types of curriculum design are as follows:

Discipline led: units of learning are based on traditional or contemporary academic disciplines complemented by vocational units (liturgy, ministry, placements etc.) Units within a discipline-based curriculum can of course include intentionally multi-disciplinary units that draw on a number of named disciplines, but the intention would still be to work with the approaches of particular disciplines.

Thematic: curricula constructed around theological-vocational themes in which the necessary disciplinary knowledge is introduced as needed. Thematic curricula tend to have an in-built integrative intention, drawing together discipline-related knowledge and skills with candidates' experience and formation for a particular role.

Foundation phase followed by integrated or thematic units: discipline-based units make up the foundation phase of the curriculum that is then followed by thematic units, integrating theological and vocational learning, including placements.

Portfolio: formally there is no programme or curriculum but instead a candidate has to evidence the required outcomes ('competencies'). The evidence can come from prior learning or from units of learning drawn from a number of providers or sources.

Other possibilities that may be common to a number of approaches, for example the 'spiral' theory of learning in which the candidates return to important themes and/or disciplines but at a higher level and so consolidate and build on their learning.

Other possibilities not yet used in overall curriculum design: **problem-based learning** (presenting a pastoral or theological issue in practice and then enabling the candidate to explore the theological, vocational and pastoral learning which are needed to tackle the 'problem').

The different models are not mutually exclusive, and we have observed that in practice curriculum design in pre-ordination training varies according to two axes: theory–practice, and disciplinary–interdisciplinary.

A Disciplinary Theoretical	B Interdisciplinary Theoretical
Curriculum design according to the traditional theological disciplines – teaching and assessment is primarily led by the interests of subject specialists.	Curriculum design that cuts across disciplinary boundaries – teaching and assessment primarily led by the interests of the academy.
e.g. An introduction to the Old Testament that covers content, methods of study, examined by 2 essays which deal with historical-critical and theological issues within the OT	e.g. An introduction to the 'Bible in the Modern World' that approaches both the Bible as a cultural product which can only be understood through a combination of critical approaches to the text with an assessment of its impact on communities of readers – examined in a traditional essay format
A course on Psychology of Religion which introduces the discipline of psychology and its relevance to aspects of religion like conversion, prayer, faith development.	A course on 'Body, Self and Society', which brings doctrinal, historical, and social scientific resources to bear on questions of Christian identity and spirituality – examined in traditional essay format.

C Disciplinary Practical	D Interdisciplinary Practical
Curriculum design according to the theological disciplines – teaching and assessment is primarily led by the use to which the discipline will be put in ministry	Curriculum design that crosses disciplinary boundaries – teaching and assessment primarily led by the model of ministry to which the educational institution subscribes.
e.g. An Introduction to the OT which gives an overview of content and methods, examined by the writing of a sermon on an OT text and a paper on the value of reading the OT within church services	e.g. An introduction to the OT which focuses on issues of communal living and is integrated into a broader course framework which addresses 'the nature of our common life' from a variety of perspectives, including neighbourhood profile and placement. Assessment of the OT component by the production of a study guide to one of the prophets aimed at the local church and community.
A course on 'Pastoral Conversation', which introduces psychological concepts with particular reference to the experience of pastoral ministry, and includes attention to issues of boundaries and appropriate professional behaviour.	A course on 'the nature of the individual person' which combines attention to the doctrine of humanity and the biblical image of God with insights from pastoral psychology and attention to issues like loss and bereavement counselling and appropriate ethics for pastoral practice.

Recent validation submissions from colleges, courses and schemes suggest that very few follow model D and are thoroughly integrative throughout. Many begin with a combination of A and C, and move towards B and D as they progress. When regions think through new patterns of IME embracing pre- and post-ordination there may be shifts in the focus and method of integration, but the Learning Outcomes point to some key principles:

1   'Theoretical' and 'practical' learning takes place throughout and requires integration throughout the process. The Learning Outcomes do not validate a model of restricting 'academic' learning to the pre-ordination phase and practically based learning to the post-ordination phase.

2   A balance is required between the different kinds of learning, formation and training at every point.

3   Traditional theological disciplines will be in evidence at all stages of IME though with varying emphases and clear evidence of progression in learning.

Integration

These questions lead into issues of integration, what is meant by this, and how or where it happens. The 1992 ABM report *Integration and Assessment* is worth investigation by theological educationalists, since it offers a very helpful typology of integration. It sees four principal types of integration which are of relevance in ministerial formation.

1   Subject integration – drawing connections between different sub-disciplines within the overall field of theology;

2   Integration of theory and practice – the attempt to merge the horizons of the theological study with those of ministerial practice;

3   Integration of previous experience with the experience of training;

4   Personal integration – a developing awareness and self-understanding, which incorporates the full range of being, knowing and doing in readiness to begin ordained ministry.

Integration and Assessment comments that 'the first two types of integration are limited in their effectiveness unless they are also supported by emphasis upon how learning takes place in the individual's awareness and self-understanding' (p. 51) The third and fourth categories of integration therefore come into play as an essential part of the journey towards ordained ministry and as IME continues in ministerial practice.

We think this leads to some further important principles for curriculum designers:

1   There is a strong case for experiential learning to be foundational, especially in relation to the traditional theological disciplines, so that issues of personal and spiritual formation are engaged from the beginning.

2   The Learning Outcomes have 'reflective practitioners' as a primary quality and skill for ministry, so there is a strong case for establishing theological reflection skills as a means in integrative studies.

3   If flexibility is not to mean individualism then it is important to establish from the beginning not only individual learning style preferences but also collaborative learning styles, so that candidates and ministers work both within their preferred styles and outside of them.

4   Personal and experiential integration is part of the whole programme, not an added extra to an academic or HE validated programme. This does not mean that everything has to be assessed, marked and accredited but it does mean that the assessment procedures for making judgements about the whole person are operative throughout the programme. There needs to be further consideration about how this kind of reporting process will be undertaken

and sustained over the new IME. It may be that this is not simply a matter of extending the annual reporting currently in operation for pre-ordination, but instead to focus such reporting in the year prior to ordination, and in the year prior to completion of IME.

Assessment

Whether it is loathed or welcomed, assessment is major feature on the landscape of both higher education and preparation for ministry programmes. In the IME context, there are usually two different but related frames of assessment working side by side: (1) academic assessment, linked to formal accreditation and the gaining of awards, and (2) Church assessment, judgements made Church bodies or authorities to determine a person's readiness and ability to exercise a ministry. While these two parallel structures and process are sometimes complementary and sometimes in tension, a definition of assessment as 'processes of getting information and communicating it to people so that they can make judgements and decisions' holds true for both. The issue is not whether assessment will take place – universities, churches and learners depend on it – but in what form it will happen, how well will it be done and with what effect on learners, institution and church.

In any discussion about the role of assessment in the curriculum, we need to acknowledge at the outset the significant role of assessment in shaping of learning. With the increased transparency of assessment processes, published assessment criteria and the possibility of appeal in academic institutions, let alone the need to negotiate relational dynamics, students are often strategically oriented to assessment rather than teaching. This may have always been so but is now more possible and more explicit. Thus assessment structures have massive potential to form learning patterns and influence life long models of learning. Utilized positively, assessment can enhance learning and integrate knowledge and skills, attitudes and character. However, the thoughtless or unreflective adoption of convenient patterns may undermine learning and distort outcomes.

Curriculum design needs to take these issues seriously, and we provide further stimulus for debate in Appendix 2.

Accreditation

The normal expectation is for ordinands to have gained a minimum of diploma (level 2) qualifications at the point of ordination. This accreditation should be gained for the whole programme, not simply for 'academic' elements. This is not to say that every element is or ought to be assessed through HE criteria, but that the award takes full account of the vocational nature of the education and training, with the integration of being, knowing and doing as fundamental. We believe that there are positive reasons for accreditation remaining normal in the post-ordination phase of IME. Although there is no requirement that those completing IME and moving to a post of responsibility will be graduates, the formal expectations of their skills, understanding and professional work fits level 3 criteria. Provided that accreditation is sympathetic to the integrated, vocational and professional education and training required, there is a strong case to be made for accreditation. Trainee ministers will experience recognizable continuity across the threshold of ordination for accreditation, so this level of recognition in this form adds incentive and value to learning, affirming its quality and aiding confidence in the wider society.

Quality and accountability

At present training institutions that prepare candidates for ordained ministry are inspected and their programmes validated quinqennially in an ecumenical process that is complemented by an annual moderation procedure. The implications of reconfiguring IME to incorporate pre- and post-ordination education and training are that these procedures be extended to the new style IME, i.e. to the pre- and post-ordination phases of training. This proposal was formally stated in the report of 2003 and included in the General Synod in the motion it passed in July 2003 (Proposal 14 ii). Clearly the processes will need to be reviewed to make sure that they are appropriate for the new context of regional partnerships (see below). However, with the report of 2003, we continue to recommend that the quality and accountability processes are the same for the whole of new IME, pre and post-ordination. We believe this to be important for several reasons:

- **Standards in training**: The common learning outcomes are an agreed framework for the curriculum, and therefore a mechanism is needed for assuring the sponsoring churches that the programmes offered are fit for purpose in enabling these outcomes to be met, and that the providers of training are capable of delivering them. Some form of quality and accountability process is needed to ensure country-wide standards are maintained by all, even though the practices around these have to be reviewed to make these instruments suitable in a new context.

- **Common ownership of training**: The process currently required for validation provides a framework and discipline for collaborative working and common ownership, not only of programmes but of the rationale and contexts that shape them. A well-conducted validation process strengthens an institution by helping it to be clear about what it is doing and why it is doing it. We believe that in the context of the new opportunities presented by the reconfiguring of IME the need for common ownership of programmes and their rationale, the collaboration that is needed for this ownership, will be strengthened and facilitated by a process that embraces the whole of IME.

- **The catholic context of training**: Trainers are accountable to the sponsoring churches, and not just to their regions. Validation, Moderation and Inspection are means by which regions, and institutions within them are located in a catholic context of the churches. Such instruments are means of ensuring that there is commonality of purpose between regions, and a means of sharing good practice and facilitating convergence where this is helpful (as for example happened in the1992 ABM report *Integration and Assessment*, or the 1999 report *Stranger in the Wings*).

- **Bringing current IME and current CME practitioners within one framework**: As noted earlier in this paper, all working within pre-ordination training institutions are familiar with the practices of validation, moderation and inspection; many working in post-ordination training are not. A central aim of the report was of 2003 to remove or at least bridge the fault-line that currently exists between these two phases of IME. Common practices and methodologies are one way of doing this.

Finally, we note that the whole range of quality and accountability processes (inspection, validation, moderation, Reader moderation) are currently under review to ensure that the form of these processes is appropriate to the new contexts of training. This review will be looking at the strengths of our current systems, and will seek to devise a quality and accountability framework that:

- Draws on the best of current practice;

- Helps to bridge the fault-line between current IME and current CME;

- Takes account of the new context of regional partnerships and the broader range of training being supervised by them;

- Is proportionate to the training enterprise and is realistic about the resources of the participating churches.

Shaping curriculum delivery

Curriculum designers now need to deal with two main scenarios:

1   **The pre-ordination phase in one region and the post-ordination phase in another**: where a candidate will or may move at the point of ordination, i.e. those training in a college and those training for a more widely deployable ministry on courses. (While it is convenient to refer to college or course type training, it needs to be noted that the report of 2003 also recommends more use of combinations of types of training, e.g. some part-time followed by

some full-time or vice versa.) This is clearly the more demanding challenge, as there will be more complexity. For those who are nationally deployable, the future location of training after ordination will not be known at the start of training and therefore it is more difficult to plan concretely. This might lead to the conclusion that it would be best for a candidate if possible to return to the pre-ordination training location as part of the post-ordination training package to enable continuity, but this has to be set within the broader concerns of the post-ordination phase of IME to learn contextually and in the company of a peer group who share other aspects of ministerial life. When viewed in this context it is better for the continuing training of the candidate normally to be in the region where ministry is being exercised. There will of course need to be close liaison with the training institute where the pre-ordination phase of training took place. We anticipate that in each region, with the resources and student numbers available, there will be a significant 'basket' of modules which can be utilized to ensure progression in learning and minimising of repetition. Curriculum designers must therefore be clear about not only the aims and outcomes of each module, but how this learning and experience could be used in overall packages of learning. This is required not only for coherence and integration of pathways within a region, but also for advice and information if and when a move takes place between regions.

2   **The whole of IME in one region**: where a candidate trains in the region in which he/she will minister, i.e., most course or OLM candidates and some college candidates. While most such candidates will complete their IME in the region, a few might be encouraged to draw on particular resources elsewhere – for example in another region which has developed a specialism in a particular type of ministry which is appropriate for the minister in question.

Within this four 'typical pathways' can be traced with some confidence for Anglican candidates.

1   A pathway for education, formation and training whose primary delivery will be dispersed and part-time over all of IME.

2   A pathway for education, formation and training whose primary delivery will be full-time in the pre-ordination phase and which will be delivered during full-time ministry in the post-ordination phase.

3   A pathway for education, formation and training whose delivery will be dispersed and part-time in the pre-ordination phase and which will be delivered during full-time ministry in the post-ordination phase.

4   A pathway for education, formation and training whose delivery will be a mixture of modes throughout IME, either through a mixed mode training programme, or through candidates moving between periods of full and part-time training within the pathways offered above.

Within this there are various possible modes of delivery to consider:

1   dispersed learning that is face to face, but as local as possible to where students/candidates live;

2   dispersed learning that is through e-learning or other forms of distance learning, which may be complemented by gathered group work;

3   gathered learning that is in regional or sub-regional groups, either for more specialized programmes, or to ensure viability of groups;

4   gathered learning that is residential in form, either for short or longer periods;

5   dispersed or gathered learning that goes beyond the region.

The development of these different pathways and the varied modes of delivery within them hold open the possibility and prospect of some creative work, and an opportunity to think 'outside the box'. Grasping this opportunity, and doing this in a larger, collaborative context with new or relatively unfamiliar partners, will present a considerable challenge to already hard-pressed personnel. The risk is also present of training institutions seizing this moment to develop entrepreneurial instincts to 'corner markets'; or of regions doing such creative work that new fault lines appear between different regions. There is the perennial danger, exhibited in current practices, where wheels are constantly reinvented.

We therefore propose that a number of initiatives are taken to minimize these risks:

1   That practitioner conferences are established in consultation between the appropriate committees of the sponsoring churches and the IME and CME networks. A series of day seminars for curriculum designers is already being planned for the Autumn of 2005.

2   That a web site is developed to complement and support the above conferences, so that practitioners can easily share good practice, and engage in ongoing debate about these issues.

3   That discussions are opened between the networks of those currently responsible for IME and for CME1–4 with a view to developing new patterns of practitioner conferences as we work together on common agendas.

The pattern of post-ordination IME

A key question for the design and delivery of IME in the post-ordination phase is how much time is allocated for continuing intentional and structured learning and reflection. The report of 2003 affirmed that the development of a sustained, effective ministry required that trainee ministers are enabled to establish the discipline of lifelong study and reflection and that the setting aside of significant time for the purpose is a proper claim on the minister's time. In this we are doing no more than catching up with other person centred professions. Moreover, with the redistribution of training between pre- and post-ordination phase, the safeguarding of time becomes vital if the essential, initial training is not to be severely compromised. Respondents in our consultation exercise urged us to be mindful of the particular situation of those who are not full time in ministry. We are conscious of the different levels of time available for training between full- and part-time trainee ministers and therefore we have sought to express a target in terms of the percentage of time available, rather than simply in days. We therefore recommend that **15 per cent of ministerial time**, whether for full- or part-time ministers, is allocated to study and reflection.

Full-time ministers

The report of 2003 recommended that full-time stipendiary ministers should have one day for IME per week. *In practice, taking account of holidays and other commitments, we believe that around 40 days should be allocated for intentional and structured learning and reflection, which is, of course, held within the total experience of ministry and training. In terms of our guideline above, 40 days is equivalent to 13 per cent of ministerial time, once proper allowance (nine weeks) has been made for holidays and for the particular demands of Christmas and Easter.*

Given that the five types of learning continue in this phase of IME curriculum designers again need to attend to how these will be balanced in the available time. Twenty-five per cent of this time should be allocated to formal theological learning which will often be at a college or course within the region, because of the need for continued theological study within a community of theological learning. Other kinds of learning need to be recognized: for example logged independent study, individual and/or collaborative projects, residentials, placements.

Ministers who are part time

The report of 2003 recommended that for self-supporting ministers who are part time a pattern of engagement similar to that of a dispersed pre-ordination phase should continue. A possible configuration could be something like:

- 20 evenings per year

- 1 x 5 day residential

- 3 study days

Although part-time ministers have less time available, and there will be a range in terms of their availability, the goal of attending to the equivalent of 30–40 credits of learning a year is attainable within the above configuration, enabling part-time trainee ministers to complete IME within the timescale of a first appointment. However, they may take longer to satisfy the additional criteria to take up a post of responsibility. We believe that this is an important aspect of flexibility, and regions should be encouraged to provide more varied and creative pathways for the diverse patterns of availability.   Although the time available to full- and part-time trainee ministers varies, it is important that the curriculum is designed to maximize the opportunity for learning in the post-ordination phase to be shared together, requiring at times full-time trainee ministers to yield to the availability of their part-time colleagues.

Pathways and destinations

It will be crucial that in each region, the various officers and institutions work together to produce a coherent approach to formation for the trainee minister which takes account of prior learning and the specified focus of ministry. They need to establish clear lines of accountability and reporting so that key decisions about readiness for ordination and wider responsibility can be made by the appropriate bodies. The theological model of partnership as covenanted members of the body of Christ, outlined at the start of this report, will take time to embody in practice but will bring benefits both to those training, those engaged in formation and the wider Church.

The version of this report circulated in December 2003 assumed a relatively firm structure of an RTP, with enough institutional shape to enable it to make informed and consensual decisions about training pathways, or to be able to make clear recommendations to sponsoring churches. Subsequent developments suggest that the organization of regional partnerships will be varied and in many cases deliberately 'light touch'. It is therefore less likely that the kind of working relationships envisaged above will be possible or appropriate, at least in the initial stages of working regionally. However, we are also very aware that there is increasing flexibility of training pathways offered by and in existing institutions and that already decisions need to be taken about training pathways that involve all the participants: working with emerging regional structures simply makes this more explicit. Therefore, we suggest some possible procedures that are needed now, but which will be increasingly needed in the future.

- Pathways for IME will be shaped by at least five factors or pressures:

    o The prior experience and learning that a candidate brings. Therefore, transparent and robust procedures need to be developed for APL/APEL which can be affirmed by training institutions within an regional partnership as well as HE institutions that will accredit ministerial training and formation.

    o The intended or envisaged ministerial deployment – local ministry or locally or nationally deployable.

    o The circumstances of the candidate in terms of their present time availability for training, and the ways in which this could or should change in the light of their vocation and ministry.

    o The requirements of sponsoring churches and the need to evidence that the learning outcomes have been met at each phase.

    o The need for stable and coherent cohorts in which ministerial and personal formation can take place, a need which is important not only for the candidates, but also for training institutions.

- The above suggests that for Anglicans there could be a termly meeting of regional DDOs, Principals of training institutions and/or their Directors of Studies; and CME officers/Directors of Ministry in order to:

    o Examine the needs and opportunities of emerging candidates, and to do this at the earliest possible stage so that theological education and training can be an integral part of the process of discernment of vocation;

    o To outline preferred training pathways and the relationship of the candidate to the institutions within the region, and to facilitate a process between the candidate, the DDO and the training institutions to arrive at an agreed pathway. For some this pathway can be given in reasonably full and clear form – for example for a non-deployable candidate who will remain in the region for the whole period of IME; for others the outline will be less complete, but nonetheless clear enough to enable coherent decisions to be made about the pre-ordination phase of training and formation.

    o To be clear about where oversight and responsibility for the candidate is to be located, and how this will be carried out;

    o To prepare and submit applications for APL/APEL according to agreed procedures;

    o To monitor and moderate decisions about training pathways in the context of ensuring the viability and stability of cohorts within training pathways;

    o To make these decisions aware of funding implications for the churches and the training institutions;

    o To make recommendations to sponsoring bishops.

Other sponsoring churches, where students and candidates relate differently to the local, regional and national church are invited to explore whether the above is a useful practice for them, or what mechanisms can be developed to ensure that the same issues are addressed.

Readiness for ordination or post of responsibility

The normal expectation is that trainee ministers will be eligible to take up appointment as incumbent or other first responsibility position or (in the cases of NSMs and OLMs) further appointments when they have completed all of the elements of the agreed IME programmes that apply to them, other than in exceptional circumstances.

At present the formal mechanism for establishing whether a person should continue in training, or proceed to ordination, is through the end of year report compiled by the training institution. There seems no obvious reason for changing a well established and understood process, except that this would need to be extended into the post-ordination phase of IME. Therefore, the existing methods of reporting in this phase would need to be brought into a formal relationship with all the partner institutions who were involved in their continuing education, training and formation. Reporting in both the pre-ordination and post-ordination phase would need to be related clearly to the agreed learning outcomes and their satisfactory completion.

If for any reason changes are made to agreed pathways within a region this must be clearly agreed by the parties concerned, and the new training pathway designed with the same rigour as the first.

We assume that a candidate will not be appointed to a post of responsibility until it is reported that the agreed learning outcomes have been completed through the completion of an agreed pathway of training. If for some unavoidable reason this does not happen – for example post-ordination training is interrupted by a move to another region brought about by a change in a partner's work – then appropriate arrangements should be made with the receiving diocese/district/synod and regional partnership – for completion of training within a specified timescale.

Formal structures of oversight

The report of 2003 contains the statement that 'our ministers will be expected to respond to contemporary demands for professional competence within ministry – while representing the discipleship of one who walks with Jesus Christ' (p. 47). The fulfilment of such demands, which are increasingly the norm in our society, requires training for the clergy themselves and an assurance that such training has been given. Without agreed learning outcomes or capability processes, bishops and others in positions of responsibility are in the difficult position of assuring the wider community that a minister is fit to practice, whilst they have no secure demonstrable knowledge that this is the case.

We note that the Review of Clergy Terms of Service report in the Church of England (p. 46) makes a clear recommendation for the introduction of formal capability procedures within the Church. 'The principal concerns of a capability procedure should be to help people to improve and deal with problems of poor performance before they become too serious to be remedied. It is about ensuring that people have been made fully aware what is required of them and have been given opportunity – through training and other means – to equip themselves with the resources to improve their performance . . .' We believe that our own work, especially the Learning Outcomes, could contribute to the addressing of poor performance which the capability procedure is designed to address and propose that further work be done to explore this.

There may be a danger in the future of action being taken against a bishop as a consequence of the actions of someone who lacked proper training for the license they held. With capability procedures in place there is the likelihood that a curate may face capability procedures where it is believed that their training had been lacking.

This leads us to the recommendation that the Church work towards an agreed level of capability for its ministers that is determined at the completion of IME. In some cases the IME period may need to be longer. For example an NSM who is able to offer very limited time to the parish or someone who has suffered a difficult curacy might expect to spend more years in the post-ordination phase of IME before it could be determined that they have fulfilled the Learning Outcomes. We also note that the Learning Outcomes can be used to determine training needs when transfer is sought between different types of ministry and to determine a person's capability to undertake a new form of ministry.

Section 4

The learning environment of the trainee minister

It is the vision of *Formation for Ministry within a Learning Church* that there should be considerable continuity between the learning that takes place for the student minister/ordinand in the pre-ordination theological institution and in the post-ordination phase including the local context for ministry occasioned by a first appointment. Nevertheless, once the locus for training is primarily a local church environment, particular dynamics come into play. The dynamics of this first experience of public ministry vary according to denominational practice and theology. For URC ministers the first experience of public ministry under supervision is the internship. After ordination the URC minister receives very little close supervision. For Methodist presbyters and deacons, the first appointment involves a considerable degree of responsibility, and often for probationer presbyters the pastoral charge of churches, but under the supervision of the Superintendent Minister. For Church of England curates, there is closer supervision for a longer period. However, in each case, the learning environment of the training minister will have a number of facets:

1   The local context for ministry;

2   The formal structures of oversight within the relevant denomination;

3   The training incumbent/superintendent/supervising minister and others working with the newly ordained;

4   Continued formal engagement in IME, normally within the region;

5   Peer groups of those engaged in similar formal studies and at similar stages of ministry, within the denomination and ecumenically;

6   Accountable relationships which are not part of the training framework.

We turn to a more specific discussion of some of the people and institutions involved above.

The local ministry context: parish, circuit, church, workplace

All ministerial education is contextual because the communities in which patterns of Christian living are being shaped crucially also shape ministry. The context may be recollected from personal life-experience, imaginatively reconstructed from the setting of Scripture or be the church or theological college/course/scheme community itself. However, in the post-ordination phase of IME the trainee minister is rooted in a parish, and expected to have a deep engagement with the worshipping, learning Christian community. This community provides the raw, intractable features of human experience with which Christian faith and thought must interact and against which pastoral and ministerial learning is initiated, tested and refined. Where the local context is regarded as the source of theology and not merely the recipient of theology learnt elsewhere, it is less likely that that theology will be unlearnt or discarded. The experience gained through being part of a developing faith community and network offers the material for the probationer/trainee minister and the newly ordained to make connections between theology, prayer and practice, to learn to act in a public and representative role and to grow into the role of the ordained. Since this ministerial context is crucial for continued learning the context must be carefully chosen and prepared. The local church must understand itself to be an active, not passive, agent in the training of its ordained. Good practice exists but needs to be shared further and developed (see criteria in *Beginning Public Ministry*). We offer in Appendix 3 further reflections on criteria for selecting training churches.

The formal structures of oversight and supervision within partner churches

Although our partner churches have different practices for overseeing and supervising those in the early years of ministry, there needs to be clarity about the formal lines of responsibility and accountability operative within the churches, and the roles of various officers and personnel who contribute. In the Church of England, responsibility lies with bishops who share this with two key people: a CME officer and a training incumbent. **The CME officer** (or equivalent) has formal responsibility for ensuring that the overall pathway and provision of post-ordination training, in partnership with the regional partnership, is in place and properly supervised. This will include ensuring that a full training plan and agreement with the trainee minister, training minister, local church and regional partnership is drawn up, implemented and monitored. **The training incumbent** is responsible for the day to day oversight and direction of the work of the newly ordained. A key responsibility for the CME officer is to ensure that the trainee minister is being properly supervised and that the relationship between the trainee minister and the training incumbent is itself supervised to enable it to be an effective learning environment.

The training incumbent/superintendent/supervising minister and others working with the newly ordained

- The training incumbent/minister has a crucial role in directing the work of the newly ordained, modelling good practice, providing support and challenge, enabling learning and fostering creative development that is foundational for future ministry. Such people need careful selection, training and support, and we offer some reflections on criteria for this in Appendix 4. In particular, we strongly recommend that training ministers should have formal training and possibly also a qualification in supervision skills. We offer further comment on this in Appendix 5.

- The training incumbent/minister cannot be and do everything. Unless the training incumbent/minister has the above theological and supervisory skills we strongly recommend that the work of the training minister should be complemented and enhanced by a Practical Theology work supervisor, who will work with the trainee minister during a formative period as an experienced practical theologian. In addition, there are further supervisory roles and tasks in this formative period:

  o supervising the relationship between the trainee and training minister;

  o providing an independent point of reference on the trainee minister's development and ministry;

  o providing continuity if a training incumbent/minister leaves or is absent for a prolonged period

  In some cases it may be the CME officer who undertakes some of this work, but in all cases it is the CME officer's (or equivalent) responsibility to ensure that all the above roles and tasks are met. In the case of some trainee ministers whose sending church is also their training church, the training incumbent/minister will not necessarily have been selected according to their suitability for this role. This makes the appointment of a practical theology work supervisor even more significant. In addition, for OLM candidates, there will usually be a Ministry Leadership Team which shares responsibility for the training as well as the support of the OLM.

- Other ministers, leaders and members in the local church, lay and ordained have gifts, skills and experience which can often be overlooked in a narrowly focused 'training relationship'. Some will have particular expertise in the development of ministerial gifts, from theological reflection and experience in preaching to management skills and voice production. Some will carry the 'birth story' and folk memory of the church which it will be important to appreciate if clergy are to be attuned to the church's background history. Others will be able to provide an introduction into welfare, educational, industrial and communal institutions within the environment. Wardens, Stewards and Elders will have a particular role in explaining the responsibilities they fulfil in the church, the management of change, the relationship between clergy and laity and reflections on different leadership styles. Lay members should make a contribution to the review and assessment of curates as currently happens in Methodist practice in relation to Worship Development Groups. Where parishes have Ministerial Leadership Teams there will be an opportunity to work and learn collaboratively in promoting the vision and mission of the church. More generally, lay members should have opportunity to offer critical-supportive feedback to the clergy. All of this emphasizes that the local church is an active partner in the training process, and therefore itself needs proper preparation.

Theological institutions within regional partnerships

It is fundamental to the report of 2003 that, alongside training incumbents/ministers and CME officers, theological institutions within regional partnerships will be involved throughout IME, and, although their involvement is likely to be greater at the pre-ordination phase, they will continue to be involved in the post-ordination phase. The role of module tutors within the regional partnership needs to be recognized in the overall tutorial, supervisory and support provision for a trainee minister.

Peer Groups

Learning takes place in a variety of overlapping peer groups. Careful thought needs to be given in the design of curriculum to the learning and formational needs in which groups and intentional cohorts make a significant contribution. Lack of thought at this point will either multiply groups in which the trainee is involved which would result in loss of focus and effectiveness, or have groups that are not well designed for their purpose. For example, trainee ministers could be involved in three significant learning groups and cohorts:

- The group in which formal learning takes place in the continuing engagement with theological study, which will probably be ecumenically mixed, and have a variety of different types of learners present. This may have 'knowing' as a focus.

- A regional (or sub-regional) cohort of ministers in the same of similar phase of their vocational journey, which may be ecumenical for at least some of its work. This may have 'doing' as a focus in terms of developing ministerial skills and practice.

- A 'local' – diocesan/district/synod – cohort, which may be denominational and offer something more like a 'cell group' environment. This may have 'being' as a focus in terms of personal, spiritual, vocational formation.

Many dioceses/districts/synods cooperation already are in or are developing partnerships in order to form effective cohorts for various purposes. While responsibility for the post-ordination phase is vested with these bodies, the planning and purpose of these activities must be undertaken in the regional partnership, otherwise the central vision of the report of 2003 for synergy, continuity and integration will be lost.

Joint clergy–Reader learning

Where there is shared learning between trainee ministers and Readers there is likely to be greater trust and effectiveness in the practical exercise of ministry. Moreover the opportunity for trainee ministers to forge their theology with lay members representing life work context, forces a deeper engagement with the prevailing community and contributes to reconnecting them with the neglected world of work. At the same time, full-time clergy will also have additional needs of their own which should be addressed.

Placements

Church and social placements/attachments are required in pre-ordination training, and are common in preparation for the discernment of vocation. Whilst there is a limit to the range of experiences that can be provided at this stage, some additional placements or supplementary church attachments are usually needed to provide opportunities for further development in areas not provided within the training parish itself. It will also be important to gain experience of different styles or worship or of particular spheres of ministry, for example occasional offices where these are not available in the home church. In the Church of England the arrangement of sharing a curate between parishes or curate exchanges between parishes can have the same effect. Placements can also serve to help the minister relate to the church at a wider level, engendering solidarity and identity with the Church as a whole. Similarly, visits to international agencies, such as the World Council of Churches, or to overseas linked dioceses, widen horizons. Placements can also serve to introduce trainee ministers to one or two specialist areas of ministry that may influence them in considering the future pattern of their ministry. Placements should always be set up on the basis of clear agreed learning outcomes. The length of placements should be determined according to what is required in order to achieve desired outcomes, whilst recognizing that learning comes from being embedded in a context over a sufficient period for the pains and hurts and joys of the sphere of ministry to be shared. Being part of the management of change involves in being present for long enough for change to be seen through. Placements are a cost on time in the parish but should be set in the context of the primacy of investing in the development of the lifelong ministry of the training minister. The crucial question will be the comparative benefits for each particular trainee minister in experience, learning and development between a placement and the equivalent time spent in the parish.

External accountable relationships

We recommend that trainee ministers work with a person external to the training and reporting process in a trusting and strictly confidential basis. Some call this person a mentor (an 'experienced and trusted adviser' (OED)), or personal adviser; others may prefer to use a spiritual director or soul friend. Their role is:

- To provide a safe and objective perspective in the work situation and to help the trainee minister to gain perspective on the work they do;

- To provide a safe space in which relationships, hopes, fears, expectations and work-family-lifestyle patterns can be shared and explored.

Work-life balance and the trainee minister's work load

It is clearly vital for the trainee minister to have a good balance of real ministerial work, spiritual support, pastoral care that attends to role dynamics as well as to affective issues, and practical theology work and study supervision. Together these will make a major contribution to the professional development of the trainee minister as an ordained minister of the wider Church as well as a minister who serves in a particular local church. We offer some reflections in Appendix 6 about 'The pattern of the trainee Minister's working life' and the minister's workload.

Realizing the vision

It is essential that the vision of the report of 2003 is enthusiastically communicated not merely as a shift of process but a profound change in people's hearts and minds. The potential benefits for the Church's mission, of providing well-resourced, coherent, intentional, formation, learning opportunities for the whole people of God, has been indicated above. Here we indicate in summary the 'selling points' resulting from the proposals as they relate to the different constituencies.

Trainee ministers

- Supervised/coached by a training incumbent/minister who has met the required professional expertise;

- Encouraged to develop a habit of reflective practice on ministry that recognizes and integrates prior learning;

- Assisted to form a balanced lifestyle consisting of ministerial practice, reflection, prayer, study and Sabbath rest and recreation;

- Encouraged to maintain academic interests and to pursue specialist study if appropriate;

- Enriched by shared, purposeful ecumenical collaboration.

Training incumbents/supervising ministers

- Encouraged to develop and hone coaching skills and experience within the supervisory relationship;

- Resourced and with opportunity for growth in confidence through involvement in the regional partnership;

- Stimulated to regular review and reflection and investment in personal and professional development through challenging collegial relationships.

Training church

- A training church has the incentive to take seriously the vocation to learn, reflect and review as a dimension of Christian discipleship;

- The way trainee ministers take their own learning seriously becomes the catalyst and model for lay Christians in a parish to take seriously their own learning and formation;

- Trainee ministers encourage local churches to reconsider the rationale and practice of their established traditions and patterns in the light of recent developments in pastoral praxis;

- Local churches have the satisfaction of providing a learning environment that lays foundations for a person to exercise a lifetime's ministry in the wider Church;

- A training church will enable its congregation to develop skills in critical-supportive feedback.

Developing the conditions for a trainee minister's learning

The training minister/incumbent has a key role in shaping and directing the work of the trainee minister. Carefully thought out domains of learning, progression in opportunities for experience, should be explicit in the training plan developed with the CME officer. We offer some reflections on some of these domains:

- *Some explicit skills based training*: trainee ministers will come with some transferable skills and some skills that are not appropriate to the local ministry context. Some help will need to be given in discernment and development in this area. Other skills will need to be learned afresh. It involves skill as well as knowledge and spirituality, for example, to chair an effective church meeting; to pray with someone in need; to conduct a marriage well. Intentionally teaching skills is part of the supervision that training ministers need. Precise needs and who should deliver the training will vary across denominations as well as between individual context.

- *A context in which the training minister may develop as a minister and leader*: Training ministers/incumbents need to provide planned and incremental opportunities for trainee ministers to lead, enabling them to take responsibility, under supervision, for key areas of ministry and mission and to initiate new projects, helping them to analyse and evaluate them.

- *Time and space to learn and grow from others and in other contexts*: the training minister/incumbent plays a key role in enabling training to take place both within the context where the training minister is appointed, and in the wider networks and partnerships through academic institutions and peer groups, diocesan/district/synod IME provision, ecumenical partners. This means that the whole curacy/probation/internship will need to be structured around the training needs of the training minister rather than the needs of the local church.

- *Supportive and constructive feedback*: interns, probationers and curates are working under supervision. Increasingly they should be able to work independently and exercise a leadership role. This role must be supported by intentional time given to helping them reflect upon their role and their embodiment of that role. Regular time should be set aside, not for staff meetings in the sense of planning events together, nor for prayer, in the sense of saying the office together – though both of these are important. This means time set aside to think explicitly about how the trainee minister is progressing and should focus upon the learning outcomes as they relate to ministerial work. Work of this kind is skilled and demanding, particularly when training ministers play other roles as colleague, person in oversight, fellow disciple and sometimes, friend. This is why we strongly recommend formal training and qualification for training ministers, and why we recommend that further supervision outside the immediate training relationship is provided through the CME officer (or equivalent) and/or the Practical Theology work supervisor.

- *Reporting*: good practice needs to be developed about formal reporting in this phase of training that build upon the experience of those in pre-ordination training and which is designed to gather the necessary evidence to enable robust recommendations to be made to responsible bodies about progress, satisfactory completion of IME and fitness to exercise ministry in a post of responsibility.

Financing of stipendiary trainee minister posts

Because of the enhanced nature of the post-ordination phase of IME potential training parishes and other local churches are likely to have strong views about taking responsibility for funding stipendiary trainee minister posts. The funding of IME is properly the responsibility of the whole Church, not just of local churches that provide the contexts for the post-ordination phase of IME. Indeed, good quality IME partner churches may be lost as training resources if having a trainee minister is seen as imposing unfairly an additional financial burden. Furthermore, it is clearly desirable for the Church to provide trainee minister posts in a variety of contexts, including rural ministry and inner city ministry settings, including settings that foster new ways of being church.

APPENDICES

Appendix 1 – for the Methodist Church

The main emphases of this report are in continuity with themes in the development of training for ordination in Methodist practice:

- the aspiration to understanding formation for ministry as a seamless robe across foundation, pre-ordination training and probation;

- the establishment of common learning objectives/assessment criteria that will give a connexional framework for training.

Given the numbers of Methodists who train on courses with a majority of Church of England students, the development of an ecumenically common framework of learning objectives is helpful in achieving a connexional strategy. Potentially the establishment of regional partnerships will mean that there will be a coherent framework within which District Probationers' Secretaries and theological institutions can work together to achieve a seamless robe for student ministers and probationers.

The recommendation to the Church of England in this report is that IME should take around seven years (two to three years before ordination and four years after it). This is not an arbitrary figure but one arrived at from experience of how long it takes to form identity and develop the skills and deep knowledge necessary to be equipped for significant responsibility as an ordained person. Although no easy equation can be made between the responsibilities exercised by Incumbents and Superintendent Ministers, those Methodists involved in the devising of the Learning Outcome believe that the skills, character and knowledge required of both are sufficiently comparable to warrant similar training. The pathway which Methodists will take towards this *telos*, however, will be different. Key questions to bear in mind include:

- The shape of foundation training (IME1) and the impact of any review;

- The competencies needed of those ready to be stationed (by the end of IME 3) and how these differ from those required of an Anglican about to be ordained deacon;

- The competencies needed of those ready to be ordained and received into full connexion;

- The overall length of time that currently is allowed to Methodist formation;

- The attention and contexts in which presbyters are currently trained for Superintendency and wider oversight.

Current Methodist practice

The table below sets out the current Methodist learning outcome statements and timetable for formation. This table should be compared with the Learning Outcomes for the Church of England as set out in this report, and the Learning Outcomes table as formatted for the Methodist Church in the two versions below.

Methodist Outcome Statements as already agreed by the Methodist Conference

	At the point of entry into foundation training a candidate will:	By the end of an agreed foundation training programme a foundation student will: IME 1 (Foundation Training: often part time over 2 years; occasional full time 1 year)	Expected competencies for presbyters and deacons about to be stationed are: IME 2-3 (Pre-ordination training; sometimes only 1 year fulltime; sometimes 2)	Expected competences for those ready for ordination and to be received into full connexion: IME 4-5 (Probation: normally 2 years full time)
Vocation (call and commitment)	1 Be judged to have a sense of Christian vocation to exercise discipleship through some form of ordained or authorized ministry 2 Be baptized and normally a member of the Methodist church for two years 3 Accepts the discipline of the Methodist Church and assents to its doctrinal standards	1 Have observed and shared in different forms of service in the Church and be able to show from this experience, in the light of the theological studies undertaken, an understanding of ordained and other forms of ministry which have informed the personal appreciation of calling to discipleship 2 Have made a realistic appraisal of personal giftings for service and discipleship and how those giftings may be developed to be employed in the mission of God through the Methodist Church.	1 Some understanding of their own past and present roles and of what it means to bear a public role and to be and function as a presbyter or deacon 2 The ability to discern which of their previously acquired skills and experience can be incorporated into ordained ministry, which need to be modified and which should be discarded 3 A confidence in the Church and the resources to resist the temptation to retreat into a personal or purely local ministry	1 Have developed the capacity to bear the public roles and responsibilities of an ordained person and to perform credibly and maturely as a deacon or presbyter 2 Have gained experience in a variety of the specific roles that fall to a presbyter or deacon in the gathering church, the dispersing church and in the wider community beyond the church, and are able to handle them effectively

	At the point of entry into foundation training a candidate will:	By the end of an agreed foundation training programme a foundation student will:	Expected competencies for presbyters and deacons about to be stationed are:	Expected competences for those ready for ordination and to be received into full connexion:
		IME 1 (Foundation Training: often part time over 2 years; occasional full time 1 year)	IME 2–3 (Pre-ordination training; sometimes only 1 year full time; sometimes 2)	IME 4–5 (Probation: normally 2 years full time)
Being in relationship (with God, self and others)		4 Be able to describe an evolving discipline of worship, prayer and Bible study in fellowship with others, which sustains them in witness and service 5 Have a basic understanding of the importance of respect and of maintaining proper boundaries in pastoral situations	4 A developing spirituality and discipline of prayer consonant with their changing role and growth in learning 5 A developed self-awareness; an awareness of others; listening skills and basic pastoral understanding 6 Personal skills, including those involved in maintaining close relationships, standard courtesies, public politeness, financial management etc.	3 Have developed a spiritual discipline of praying alone and with others which both sustains them in the frequently isolated role of a deacon of presbyter and enables them to exercise the responsibility of praying for others

	At the point of entry into foundation training a candidate will:	By the end of an agreed foundation training programme a foundation student will:	Expected competencies for presbyters and deacons about to be stationed are:	Expected competences for those ready for ordination and to be received into full connexion:
		IME 1 (Foundation Training: often part time over 2 years; occasional full time 1 year)	IME 2–3 (Pre-ordination training; sometimes only 1 year fulltime; sometimes 2)	IME 4–5 (Probation: normally 2 years full time)
The Church's ministry in God's world		6 Be able to demonstrate an understanding of current social and ethical contexts in which Christian witness is to be lived out in acts of mercy, service and justice 7 Show a positive appreciation of the Methodist Church in its developing ecumenical relationships	7 A developing understanding of the gospel and mission of the kingdom of God; basic skills of interpretation; the ability to relate faith and experience and to begin to think theologically about their context 8 A specific understanding and experience of Methodism in its breadth and diversity and in relation to other churches	4 Have gained understanding of the imperatives of the gospel and the nature of contemporary society and skills in articulating and engage in appropriate forms of mission in response to them. 5 Have developed a high level of skill in interpretation and a proven capacity to relate theology to context in a variety of situations
Leadership and collaboration		8 Have developed an understanding of how groups operate and an awareness of personal preferred styles of leadership and collaboration within the people of God	9 An understanding, experience and proven capacity to handle working with people of different gifts and abilities and with various responsibilities in the life of the Church and the work of the kingdom [including some who are not chosen or approved by the student], and to exercise leadership as and when appropriate.	6 Have gained experience in handling issues of power and authority 7 Are able to act independently but collegially with other ministers and with the community of the whole Church

	At the point of entry into foundation training a candidate will:	By the end of an agreed foundation training programme a foundation student will:	Expected competencies for presbyters and deacons about to be stationed are:	Expected competences for those ready for ordination and to be received into full connexion:
		IME 1 (Foundation Training: often part time over 2 years; occasional full time 1 year)	IME 2–3 (Pre-ordination training; sometimes only 1 year fulltime; sometimes 2)	IME 4–5 (Probation: normally 2 years full time)
Learning and understanding	Be capable of benefiting from and completing a foundation training programme of study	9 Be able to show a basic knowledge of the Bible and representative Christian texts and know how the have been understood and used by the Church in its missionary task	10 A firm and thorough grounding in the basic content of theological, biblical, historical, liturgical, missiological and social and pastoral studies and in the basic skills of handling such material 11 A proven ability in applying the relevant bodies of knowledge appropriately to particular situations	8 Have developed a working knowledge and understanding of the Constitutional Practice and Discipline of the Methodist Church and an expertise in applying it practice.
Communication		10 Have an understanding of communication in worship and learning in groups and demonstrate the ability to take part in the leadership of worship as required in a local church or group 11 Have practised listening skills in relating to others, be able to express thoughts clearly in speech, to use simple techniques of communication, and be able to make positive use of feedback and assessment	12 An understanding of worship and of liturgical principles, and the ability to lead worship as required in a variety of styles 13 A basic understanding of preaching, hermeneutical principles and techniques of communication, and an ability to preach in a number of styles and contexts and to make positive use of feedback and assessment	9 Have learnt to work under discipline and to make effective use of supervision

Foundation Training (IME 1) This is normally two years part time (or more usually 18 months) and sometimes one year full time. The learning objectives set out for the successful completion of Foundation Training include some of those named in the selection criteria of the Church of England and some of those expected to be completed by the end of IME 3. This report has made the assumption that during Foundation Training a significant percentage of the learning objectives for IME 1–3 will be met, although none of those relating specifically to the formation of ministerial identity. For Methodists, these will need to receive more attention in IME 2–3.

Pre-ordination Training (IME 2–3) Pre-ordination training will focus upon the development of a presbyteral/diaconal identity and continue to work on the range of outcomes identified for IME 1–3 but begun during foundation training.

Stationing [on successful completion of the learning objectives specified for IME 1–3 which correlate quite nearly to expected competencies for those ready for stationing.]

Probation (IME 4–7) Standing Orders require that all probationers serve two years before reception in full connexion and ordination during which time they continue to be assessed and to receive designated study time. Although in many Districts there are early years in ministry groups for those in the first five years of ministry, oversight and funding and designated time for study are not normally extended beyond ordination. The learning objectives for IME 4–7, to the extent that those competencies are judged necessary for circuit ministry, need to be met and assessed during probation. Learning Objectives that relate specifically to wider responsibilities, i.e. Superintendency, would need to be addressed in another format: currently on short courses.

Questions and challenges to current Methodist practice raised by this report

Criteria for selection and assessment Currently Methodists use six categories for selection of foundation students; assessment of successful completion of foundation training; selection for ordination training; readiness for stationing; readiness for ordination. These are: vocation; being in relationship with God, self and others; the Church's ministry in God's world; leadership and collaboration; learning and understanding; communication. The common Learning Outcomes below contain very similar learning objectives but are arranged according to the nine selection criteria of the Church of England. The Methodist Church has two main options:

1   to adopt the joint Learning Outcomes as they stand *or*

2   to adopt the common Learning Outcomes and order them under our current six headings.

Option 1 represented in the table below, adopts the joint Learning Outcomes including the categories for assessment and orders them, with minor alterations for the Methodist Church. In either case there is a need to review the forms relating to selection, assessment and reporting. The first option would make ecumenical co-operation in regions easier. Forms would be mutually more intelligible although each ecumenical partner would still require reports at different stages and for different bodies of oversight.

The natural development for many presbyters and most deacons beyond ordination will be via pathways that do not lead to Superintendency but may involve the development of other specialisms. Continued formation in ministry in the two years following ordination, therefore would focus on developing these charisms. In the table below we focused on readiness for Superintendency. This mirrors the column in the Church of England table for those ready for responsibility. It does not imply that the role of a Superintendent is equivalent in straightforward terms to that of an Incumbent in the Church of England, but suggests there are skills common to both.

Joint Learning Outcomes (sample) as formatted for the Methodist Church Option 1

Ministry within the Methodist Church			
On acceptance as a candidate for ordination, having completed foundation training	At the point of stationing candidates should	At the point of ordination and reception into full connexion	In order to be ready for Superintendency
Vocation			
Be able to speak to their sense of vocation to ministry and mission, referring both to their own conviction, the statements of the Church about ordained ministry. Their sense of vocation should be obedient, realistic and informed. Show a positive appreciation of the Methodist Church in its developing ecumenical relationships.	Be able to give an account of their vocation to ministry and mission and their readiness to exercise public ministry as a probationer deacon or presbyter in the Methodist Church.	Have developed the capacity to bear the public roles and responsibilities of an ordained person and to perform credibly and maturely as a deacon or presbyter both in the Methodist Church and in the wider community.	
	Demonstrate proficiency in a range of skills and abilities needed to exercise public ministry under supervision by being able to show basic skills as a reflective practitioner;	Demonstrate proficiency in a broad range of skills and abilities needed to exercise public ministry and leadership of a local church, and the ability to do this in relatively unsupervised settings. Show developed skills as an effective reflective practitioner.	Demonstrate proficiency in the skills needed to exercise leadership and supervision of others in a position of responsibility by being able to show sophisticated skills as an effective reflective practitioner and the capacity to develop these further.
	Demonstrate familiarity with the legal, and administrative responsibilities appropriate to those appointed to public ministry and working under supervision.	Demonstrate a working understanding of and good practice in the administration of the disciplines of the Methodist Church. CPD as it relates to the local church and circuit	Demonstrate a working understanding of and good practice in the administration of the disciplines of the Methodist Church. CPD as it relates to church, circuit, district and connexional structures.
	Demonstrate ability in leading public worship and preaching, showing understanding of and good practice in liturgy and worship in settings normally encountered in circuit life and within the context of training.	Demonstrate proficiency in leading public worship and preaching, showing understanding of and good practice in liturgy and worship in a wide range of settings as appropriate to the presbyteral or diaconal role.	Demonstrate proficiency in leading public worship and preaching, showing understanding of and good practice in liturgy and worship in a wide range of settings as appropriate to the role of a team leader and one who exercises oversight.

Parameters of the curriculum and Post-ordination phase of IME

On acceptance as a candidate for ordination, having completed foundation training	At the point of stationing candidates should	At the point of ordination and reception into full connexion	In order to be ready for Superintendency
Vocation (continued)			
	Demonstrate awareness of the Church's roles and opportunities in public life and institutions, and in relation to other agencies.	Demonstrate a working understanding of the practices of Christian ministry in a range of public settings and agencies.	Demonstrate ability to take a leading role in working with other partners, representing the church in public life and other institutions.
	Show understanding of the insights and practices of other churches and traditions in worship, especially ecumenical partners.	Demonstrate engagement with ecumenical working relationships, especially with covenanting partners.	Demonstrate the ability to work ecumenically and to encourage ecumenical co-operation.
Mission and evangelism			
Demonstrate a passion for mission that is reflected in thought, prayer and action. Understand the strategic issues and opportunities within the contemporary culture. Enable others to develop their vocations as witnesses and advocates of the good news.	Participate in and reflect on the mission of God in a selected range of social, cultural and intellectual contexts in which Christian witness is to be lived in out acts of mercy, service and justice.	Participate in and reflect on the mission of God and show a developed ability to reflect consistently and imaginatively on this through a deep and intelligent engagement with Scripture and traditions of Christian thought.	Show the ability for creative leadership in enabling others to participate in the mission of God.
	Engage in and reflect upon practices of mission and evangelism, changing forms of church, and their relation to contexts and cultures.	Demonstrate engagement in mission and evangelism in a range of contexts, particularly in the local community and in relation to the local church.	Demonstrate an ability to lead and enable others in faithful witness and to foster mission-shaped churches.

Option 2 organizes the joint Learning Outcomes according to the existing six categories for formation adopted by the Methodist Conference:

Example of common Learning Outcomes as formatted for the Methodist Church Option 2

	At the point of entry into foundation training a candidate will:	By the end of an agreed foundation training programme a foundation student will:	Expected competencies for presbyters and deacons about to be stationed are:	Expected competences for those ready for ordination & to be received into full connexion:
		IME 1 (Foundation Training: often part time over 2 years; occasional full-time 1 year)	IME 2–3 (Pre-ordination training; sometimes only 1 year full-time; sometimes 2)	IME 4–5 (Probation: normally 2 years full-time)
Vocation (call and commitment)	1 Be judged to have a sense of Christian vocation to exercise discipleship through some form of ordained or authorized ministry 2 Be baptized and normally a member of the Methodist church for 2 years 3 Accepts the discipline of the Methodist Church and assents to its doctrinal standards	1 Have observed and shared in different forms of service in the Church and be able to show from this experience, in the light of the theological studies undertaken, an understanding of ordained and other forms of ministry which have informed the personal appreciation of calling to discipleship. 2 Be able to speak to their sense of vocation to ministry and mission, referring both to their own conviction, the statements of the Church about ordained ministry. Their sense of vocation should be obedient, realistic and informed. 3 Be familiar with the tradition and practice of the Methodist Church and be ready to work within them.	1 The ability to discern which of their previously acquired skills and experience can be incorporated into ordained ministry, which need to be modified and which should be discarded. 2 A confidence in the Church and the resources to resist the temptation to retreat into a personal or purely local ministry. 3 Ability to give an account of their vocation to ministry and mission and their readiness to exercise public ministry as a probationer deacon or presbyter in the Methodist Church.	1 The capacity to bear the public roles and responsibilities of an ordained person and to perform credibly and maturely as a deacon or presbyter both in the Methodist Church and in the wider community. 2 The capacity to bear a public and representative role in ministry and mission, and a readiness to exercise leadership in ordained ministry. 3 Give an account of how personal commitment to Christ and discipleship is being shaped within the roles and expectations of public ministry.

Being in relationship (with God, self and others)	At the point of entry into foundation training a candidate will:	By the end of an agreed foundation training programme a foundation student will: IME 1 (Foundation Training: often part time over 2 years; occasional full-time 1 year)	Expected competencies for presbyters and deacons about to be stationed are: IME 2–3 (Pre-ordination training; sometimes only 1 year full-time; sometimes 2)	Expected competences for those ready for ordination & to be received into full connexion: IME 4–5 (Probation: normally 2 years full-time)
		4 Be able to describe an evolving discipline of worship, prayer and Bible study in fellowship with others, which sustains them in witness and service. 5 Demonstrate good practice in a limited range of pastoral relationships, and learn from these experiences. 6 Be able to form and sustain relationships. 7 Be able to identify personal strengths and weaknesses.	4 A developing spirituality and discipline of prayer consonant with their changing role and growth in learning. 5 A developed self-awareness; an awareness of others; listening skills and basic pastoral understanding. 6 Personal skills, including those involved in maintaining close relationships, standard courtesies, public politeness, financial management etc. 7 Form and sustain relationships, both with those who are like-minded and those who differ, marked by empathy, respect and insight. 8 Demonstrate good practice in a range of pastoral relationships, and learn from these experiences. 9 Ability to exercise appropriate care of self, through developing sustainable patterns of life and work, and effective support networks.	4 Ability to form and sustain a life of prayer within the expectations of public ministry, corporate and personal worship and devotion. 5 Ability to give an account of how personal commitment to Christ is being shaped within the roles and expectations of leadership and oversight of others. 6 Ability to form and sustain relationships across a wide range of people, especially in situations of conflict and disagreement, marked by empathy, respect and insight. 7 Good practice in a wide range of pastoral and professional relationships. 8 Ability to show insight, openness, maturity and stability in the face of pressure and change and in the process of enabling change. 9 Loving service in the Church, expressed in effective and collaborative leadership, in personal discipleship, in the practice of faith and in appropriate self-care.

	At the point of entry into foundation training a candidate will:	By the end of an agreed foundation training programme a foundation student will: IME 1 (Foundation Training: often part time over 2 years; occasional full-time 1 year)	Expected competencies for presbyters and deacons about to be stationed are: IME 2-3 (Pre-ordination training; sometimes only 1 year full-time; sometimes 2)	Expected competences for those ready for ordination & to be received into full connexion: IME 4-5 (Probation: normally 2 years full-time)
The Church's ministry in God's world		6 Be able to demonstrate an understanding of current social and ethical contexts in which Christian witness is to be lived out in acts of mercy, service and justice.	10 A developing understanding of the Gospel and Mission of the Kingdom of God; basic skills of interpretation; the ability to relate faith and experience and to begin to think theologically about their context.	10 Have gained understanding of the imperatives of the gospel and the nature of contemporary society and skills in articulating and engage in appropriate forms of mission in response to them.
		7 Show a positive appreciation of the Methodist Church in its developing ecumenical relationships.	11 A specific understanding and experience of Methodism in its breadth and diversity and in relation to other churches.	11 Have developed a high level of skill in interpretation and a proven capacity to relate theology to context in a variety of situations.
		8 Demonstrate a passion for mission that is reflected in thought, prayer and action. Understand the strategic issues and opportunities within the contemporary culture. Enable others to develop their vocations as witnesses and advocates of the good news.	12 Demonstrate awareness of the church's roles and opportunities in public life and institutions, and in relation to other agencies.	12 Demonstrate engagement in mission and evangelism in a range of contexts, particularly in the local community and in relation to the local church.
		9 Engage in and reflect upon practices of mission and evangelism, changing forms of church, and their relation to contexts and cultures.	13 Show understanding of the insights and practices of other churches and traditions in worship, especially of ecumenical partners.	13 Demonstrate understanding of the imperatives of the gospel and the nature of contemporary society and skills in articulating and engaging in appropriate forms of mission in response to them.
			14 Participate in and reflect on the mission of God in a selected range of social, ethical, cultural and intellectual contexts in which Christian witness is to be lived out in acts of mercy, service and justice.	14 Demonstrate an ability to lead and enable others in faithful witness and to foster mission.
				15 Demonstrate the ability to work ecumenically and to encourage ecumenical co-operation.

	At the point of entry into foundation training a candidate will:	By the end of an agreed foundation training programme a foundation student will: IME 1 (Foundation Training: often part time over 2 years; occasional full-time 1 year)	Expected competencies for presbyters and deacons about to be stationed are: IME 2-3 (Pre-ordination training; sometimes only 1 year full-time; sometimes 2)	Expected competences for those ready for ordination & to be received into full connexion: IME 4-5 (Probation: normally 2 years full-time)
Leadership and collaboration		12 Have developed an understanding of how groups operate and an awareness of personal preferred styles of leadership and collaboration within the people of God. 13 Demonstrate effective collaborative leadership and an ability to work in teams in a limited range of settings, and learn from these experiences. 14 Demonstrate understanding of group dynamics, including the use and abuse of power. 15 Exercise appropriate accountability and responsibility in faithfully and loyally receiving the authority of others.	15 An understanding, experience and proven capacity to handle working with people of different gifts and abilities and with various responsibilities in the life of the Church and the work of the Kingdom (including some who are not chosen or approved by the student) and to exercise leadership as and when appropriate. 16 Show understanding of how children and adults learn and an ability to nurture others in their faith development. 17 Demonstrate effective collaborative leadership and an ability to work in teams in a limited range of settings, and learn from these experiences. 18 Demonstrate commitment to loving service in the Church rooted in a sustained and growing love of God, discipleship of Christ, and pilgrimage in faith in the Holy Spirit..	16 Are able to act independently but collegially with other ministers and with the community of the whole church. 17 Demonstrate appropriate use of authority in ways which enable and empower others in their mission and ministry, including colleagues. 18 Exercise effective collaborative leadership, working effectively as a member of team, and as an ordained person. 19 Demonstrate ability to support and supervise others in a limited range of roles and responsibilities. 20 Demonstrate proficiency in a broad range of skills and abilities needed to exercise public ministry and leadership of a local church, and the ability to do this in relatively unsupervised settings. Show developed skills as an effective reflective practitioner.

	At the point of entry into foundation training a candidate will:	By the end of an agreed foundation training programme a foundation student will:	Expected competencies for presbyters and deacons about to be stationed are:	Expected competences for those ready for ordination & to be received into full connexion:
		IME 1 (Foundation Training: often part time over 2 years; occasional full-time 1 year)	IME 2-3 (Pre-ordination training; sometimes only 1 year full-time; sometimes 2)	IME 4-5 (Probation: normally 2 years full-time)
Learning and under-standing	Be capable of benefiting from and completing a foundation training programme of study	16 Be able to show a basic knowledge of the Bible and representative Christian texts and know how they have been understood and used by the Church in its missionary task.	19 A proven ability in applying the relevant bodies of knowledge appropriately to particular situations.	21 Have developed a working knowledge and understanding of the Constitutional Practice and Discipline of the Methodist Church and an expertise in applying it practice.
		17 Have the necessary intellectual capacity and quality of mind to undertake satisfactorily a course of theological study and ministerial preparation and to cope with the intellectual demands of ministry.	20 A growing critical engagement with scripture and the traditions of Christian thought, characterised by faithful obedience and openness to new insights.	22 Ability to form and sustain a life of disciplined study and reflection that sustains in leadership and public ministry.
		18 Demonstrate understanding of the ways in which Christian beliefs and practices have developed in varying historical and cultural contexts.	21 Ability to form a life of study and reflection within the demands and disciplines of initial training and the expectations shaped by public ministry.	
		19 Demonstrate a growing critical engagement with scripture and the traditions of Christian thought, characterised by faithful obedience and openness to new insights.	22 Ability to interpret and use scripture across a wide range of settings, showing developed exegetical and hermeneutic skills, communicating an understanding and engagement with scripture in ways that enable others learn and explore.	
			23 Continued and disciplined engagement with Christian beliefs and practices.	

	At the point of entry into foundation training a candidate will:	By the end of an agreed foundation training programme a foundation student will: IME 1 (Foundation Training: often part time over 2 years; occasional full-time 1 year)	Expected competencies for presbyters and deacons about to be stationed are: IME 2-3 (Pre-ordination training; sometimes only 1 year full-time; sometimes 2)	Expected competences for those ready for ordination & to be received into full connexion: IME 4-5 (Probation: normally 2 years full-time)
			24 Skill as reflective practitioners, able to engage thoughtfully and critically across the spectrum of Christian tradition, in ways that deeply inform personal practices, and which enable others to learn and explore.	
			25 Ability to engage confidently with the Bible as text and as holy scripture, as skilled interpreters and communicators.	
			26 Basic awareness of and reflective engagement with beliefs, practices and spirituality of other faith traditions.	
Communi-cation		20 Have an understanding of communication in worship and learning in groups and demonstrate the ability to take part in the leadership of worship as required in a local church or group.	27 A basic understanding of preaching, hermeneutical principles and techniques of communication, and an ability to preach in a number of styles and contexts and to make positive use of feedback and assessment.	23 Have learnt to work under discipline and to make effective use of supervision.
		21 Have practised listening skills in relating to others, be able to express thoughts clearly in speech, to use simple techniques of communication, and be able to make positive use of feedback and assessment.	28 An ability in leading public worship and preaching, showing understanding of and good practice in liturgy and worship in a wide range of settings.	

A choice will need to be made between these two ways of proceeding. In either case, if the common Learning Outcomes are accepted there is a need to review the Methodist forms relating to selection, assessment and reporting. The first option would make ecumenical co-operation in regional partnerships easier. Forms would be mutually more intelligible although each ecumenical partner would still require reports at different stages and for different bodies of oversight. The second allows a greater continuity with current Methodist practice and may allow greater integrity of Methodist patterns of ministry and development.

How much time does/should formation take? The Church of England is suggesting that normally no one should become an Incumbent without six to seven years of formation. This is based on the experience that it takes time for to form an identity as an ordained person. Over the past 30 years, patterns of training for student ministers have diversified, allowing part-time and non-residential modes. If the theology of *habitus* formed in Christian community is taken seriously

- Should The Methodist Church also specify a minimum number of years over which overall formation can take place? This would mean making a parallel recommendation for the length of pre-ordination training as we have for Probation.
- How would this relate to part time formation?
- How would this be funded?
- What form should Foundation Training take and what proportion of the time allocated and of the funding should be devoted to it?

Methodist formation/ecumenical formation: In what kinds of communities should Methodist student ministers and deacons be shaped? Although Methodists are committed to training ecumenically wherever possible, the experience of many Methodist students and members of staff is that we are thinly spread across a range of training contexts, meaning that for many there is no viable Methodist peer group in formation.

- What is the value of such a peer group?
- What is an appropriate balance of Methodist formation and ecumenical engagement?
- How do we construct, maintain and fund Methodist communities of scholarship and faith in which not only generic Christian virtues and habits of theological reflection are formed, but the particular charisms of the Methodist tradition can be nurtured and critiqued and thus gifted to the wider Church?
- If it is beneficial to Methodist students and to ecumenical partners for Methodists to have a grounded and critical sense of their own identity, can the Methodist Church realistically train student ministers in every region?

What training in oversight do/should Methodists receive? The Church of England's objectives for IME 4–7 include specific objectives for exercising wider responsibility. The aim is that no-one should become an Incumbent without having met these objectives. Should the Methodist Church recognize the wisdom of identifying learning objectives specific to exercising wider responsibility and develop a programme for IME 6–7 alongside the Church of England, without successful completion of which they would not be eligible for a Superintendent's appointment. The perceived benefits of lengthening formal training beyond ordination would be to:

- Release the pressure to use the money and time available in probation to pursue particular interests rather than focusing on developing as an effective and reflective minister, for fear there will never be funding or opportunity again. Time would be released for supervision, reflective practice, retreat, spiritual direction and supported reading.

- Encourage specialization in ministry and study once generic skills have been learned by designating study time and allocating funding for courses in this period, rather than in the first two years.
- Formal accountability in supervision and study would be required beyond ordination, reducing the impression that ordination effectively leaves presbyters only loosely accountable.
- Given the demand for Superintendents and the increasing number of presbyters becoming Superintendent after five years experience who cannot have been prepared according to the more traditional apprenticeship model, IME 6–7 could provide a coherent and measured framework for developing gifts for Superintendency, allowing proper attention to be paid to the skills of leadership and the theology of oversight.

The character of probation The implications of the previous section are that probation would become heavily focused upon becoming an effective, reflective practitioner. Study would be focused upon the development of the skills and habits of ministry in collaborative groups and upon issues that arise from practice in dialogue with theological and non-theological disciplines at the level appropriate to the probationer's academic experience. Proper attention could be paid to developing particular charisms and specialisms in ministry during the post probation period of IME, involving placements, formal courses and specific further training if necessary.

Formal Supervision This report recommends that those responsible for supervising the work of those in the early years of ministry should receive some formal training in supervision. In the Church of England this particularly relates to the role of the Training Incumbent. Methodist Superintendents do not have such a close supervisory role. Nevertheless questions are raised by this report about the culture of oversight, supervision and accountability in the churches.

- Who should receive training in formal supervision within the Methodist Church? Should this include Superintendents, Placement supervisors, District Probationers' Secretaries?
- What is an appropriate theological and ecclesial model of supervision (collegial/communal/personal?) for Methodists?
- What is an appropriate model of accountability beyond probation and how is the transition managed?

The role of District Probationers' Secretaries As for the other denominations there will be particular challenges in developing curriculum for probationers. This responsibility currently lies with Districts. Many District Probationers' Secretaries have no time released from other responsibilities for this task and will be facing a change of culture in having a more formal relationship with training institutions through a regional partnership.

- Who will have over all oversight of the probationer's programme within the regional partnership?
- What is an appropriate resourcing of District Probationers' Secretaries in terms of time, training and support for new tasks?
- What is the role of a Methodist early-years-in-ministry peer group and what role is there for ecumenical groups?

Appendix 2

Assessment

Building on the main body of our report we add the following reflections

First, training for ministry needs to seek high validity forms of assessment in order nurture the intended knowledge usage in ministry in parish, circuit and church life. **Validity** is concerned with the ability of a method accurately to assess what it seeks to assess. In other words, is the tool for assessment the right one to give to evidence of the skill or knowledge we want to test? This aspect of assessment is sometimes in tension with **reliability**, the ability of a method to produce and ensure consistent standards across a range of contexts and students. Whilst all assessment methods should aim at high levels of both validity and reliability, in practice raising the standard of one is often at the expense of the other. In training for ministry high levels of validity means choosing methods most capable of judging the ability of the person to use the knowledge, skill or competence in contexts close to those required in the professional usage. For example, to use critical biblical study in preaching or systematic theology in response to questions on a radio phone-in programme, as well as in a paper for consideration at the PCC. Since, as suggested above, assessment will inevitably and profoundly shape learning, a great deal of imagination is needed to devise assessment methods that can properly test discipline-based knowledge and skill and its use in professional contexts.

The variety of methods of assessment is now wide and continually being developed. Moreover, universities and other validating authorities are likely to be responsive to creative approaches to assessment provided the rationale is clear, the criteria are robust and the intention is both to test and to strengthen learning at the appropriate level. Most such educational institutions are attuned to the needs for high validity assessment and this creates the possibility of innovative combinations in relation to the learning and assessing of theology for ministry. QAA benchmarks and performing arts assessment criteria are both useful sources for our work. Perhaps most important is attempting to hold together the forming and transforming of knowing, doing and being in those preparing for ministry. It will be tempting to seek to assess the knowledge and perhaps skills within the framework of the validated award and leave the assessing of character, spirituality and integrity to the staff in the training institution report. This should not necessarily be accepted, as ways of integrating the assessment of character, e.g. ability in reflective practice, imaginative and wise judgements and maturity in particular circumstances, can properly be part of a validated award, just as some engagement with the academic work of the learner can be part of the church's discernment processes.

Second, in curriculum design significant resources need to be allocated to assessment. If all assessment, both formative and summative, is formative of learning, then the quality of written and oral feedback is of the utmost importance, as is the time allotted to reflection and conversation to interpret and respond to feedback. This cannot be done without allowing staff sufficient time for marking, writing constructive and developmental feedback and tutorial contact. This is not just a matter of quantity but of timeliness. For feedback to be effective is needs to be close to the experience of learning and being assessed. Time allocated to contact at the right moment needs careful planning in the curriculum design and timetabling.

Self-, peer and expert assessment

Within the search for appropriate methods of assessment, a careful consideration should be given to the roles of, and balance between, self-assessment, peer assessment and the external or expert assessment of a learner. All these will figure in ongoing ministry and professional life and thus ought to be featured in early stages of training alongside each other. The balance of the elements may, however, change over the period of training so that more assessment and appraisal lies with the minister and immediate colleagues as she or he grows in experience and responsibility.

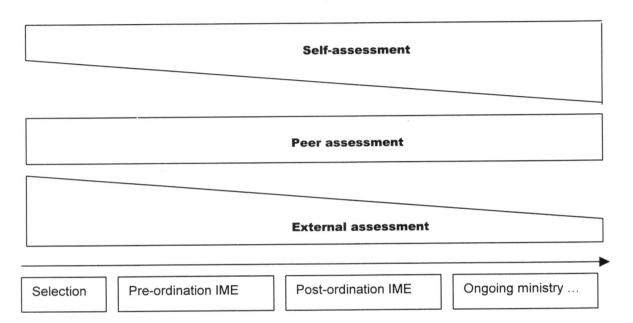

There is a good case for developing self and peer assessment practices for those in Education for Discipleship programmes, if only at an informal level, for these will act as stronger signals about the nature of learning and growth as well as laying good foundations on which to build in preparation for ministry. Assessment and appraisal of institutions and training incumbents alongside and with the help of those in training also conveys good values and nurtures a strong sense of accountability. Many training institutions have found that the end of year negotiations between tutors and learners about reports are a key part of developing self-awareness and planning for future learning needs.

Institutions usually benefit from discussing the ways in which practices and skills in self-, peer and expert assessment can be nurtured within learners and where within the curriculum these different aspects of assessment can be employed to good effect. Engaging with all forms of assessment can develop through discussion and reflection within the learning community about what criteria are appropriate and what qualities mark excellent or ideal work.

Summary

Assessment is central to curriculum design rather than an after thought to planning content and process. Assessment is consistently shown to shape profoundly the nature of learning and future patterns of engagement on the part of the learner. Hence, we need to be alert to its potential for good and ill. The suggestions made here, built on this premise, are sevenfold:

1. Devise assessment processes to test learning outcomes as they may be experienced or exercised in the role and practice of ministry.
2. Be creative and imaginative in designing assessment methods and processes in order to achieve this validity.
3. Allocate time and organize timetables for staff and students to engage at the right moments and in depth to release the learning potential of assessment and feedback.
4. Do not confine the validated assessment structures simply to knowledge or skill based learning. Seek ways of including the character and being dimensions of the intended outcomes of preparation for ministry programmes. In other words seek to integrate church and validated assessment process or at least make them overlap extensively.
5. Nurture and develop self-, peer and expert assessment throughout programmes of learning with an increase in self- and peer assessment as training develops and individuals carry more personal responsibility.
6. Engage in discussion about the nature, processes and criteria for assessment in communities of learning with all participants.
7. Encourage assessment and appraisal of all aspects of training including institutions and training incumbents with significant input from those 'in training'.

An indicative list of types of and approaches to assessment

Type	Example	Useful for
assessment of 'performance in situ'	a preacher leading a church service	assessing integration of skills, knowledge and attitudes in context
assessed written work	essay on themes in John's Gospel	assessing research, thinking and writing skills
self assessment	watching and evaluating a video of oneself in a public role	developing self reflection skills. The evaluation itself can be assessed by others
peer assessment	report on a group participation or collaborative exercise	developing and assessing self knowledge and feedback skills

Type	Example	Useful for
assessed interview or conversation	a devised pastoral encounter	testing how sensitive someone is to affective and non-verbal signals, how quickly and well people think and act on the spot
portfolio building	a collection of evidence to show one's administrative ability	assessing prior experience and competence of person in complex or diverse job
report from supervisor or mentor	a placement report	learning how your character and skills are seen by an experienced person
summary report from tutor or course leader	report to Diocesan Director of Ordinands, connexional committee or Bishop	for drawing evidence together from a variety of assessed contexts to present a whole picture of person's character and development
unseen written examinations	translating a New Testament Greek text	assessing transferable skills and ability to use knowledge and skill in 'unfamiliar' setting
assessed seminar	leading a 40-minute session on a subject topic	assessing education and communication skills as well as research and thinking ability

Some suggestions for resources for further exploration.

- For a helpful list of possible methodologies see the Oxford Brookes website at:
  http://www.brookes.ac.uk/services/ocsd/2_learntch/methods.html
- For a clearly written and practical introduction see the section on 'Assessing the Students' in: *A handbook for teachers in Universities and Colleges*, R. Cannon and D. Newble - 4th edition 2000, Kogan Page 0-7494-3181-4 (Chapter 9, pp.165–206). This offers a smaller range of methods than the list above, but is particularly useful as it suggests procedures / checklists for using different approaches.
- There is some useful material on assessment in a publication produced by the National Centre for Legal Education. Particularly interesting are the principles for assessing group work (pp. 40–42, hard copy, or 45ff. on the web version). The publication *Ensuring Successful Assessment* (£6.80) is available in PDF version on the web at www.ukcle.ac.uk/resources/bone.html, where you will also find ordering details.

For group work evaluation see:

- Published by NCLE, University of Warwick – *'Ensuring Successful Assessment'* (for details see previous bullet point) is very helpful on principles for assessing groups, with a suggested checklist of 'DOs' and 'DON'Ts'.
- Oxford Brookes University have very useful material on assessment on their website:

- http://www.brookes.ac.uk/services/ocsd/2_learntch/groupwork.html

- http://www.brookes.ac.uk/services/ocsd/firstwords/fw26.html

- http://www.brookes.ac.uk/services/ocsd/2_learntch/methods.html   (not specifically groupwork - but useful alternative assessment approaches)

- TRACE (Teaching Resources and Continuing Education) – from the University of Waterloo, Ontario, Canada – Methods for Assessing Group work with advantages and disadvantages of different approaches: http://www.adm.uwaterloo.ca/infotrac/methods.html

- http://www.nald.ca/CLR/Btg/ed/evaluation/groupwork.htm These 'Group work rubrics and checklists' offer some frameworks (and reminders) of specific things you might be on the lookout for in relation to collaborative / group work skills.

Appendix 3

Criteria for a training parish

As far as the Church of England is concerned there has been unease in recent years that the 'training parish' is such by virtue of its size and need for an extra pair of clergy hands. By contrast, almost any parish might be deemed suitable to be a 'training parish' at a particular time if it met certain criteria:

1. That it is of sufficient size, e.g. includes a range of socio-economic settings, so as to generate a sufficiently wide and demanding experience of ministry.
2. That the parish has to offer a good model of ministry, attentive to its responsibility for the wider community, and shows evidence of strategic theological thinking for its future development.
3. That the parish has the space and stability in order to undertake training at a particular juncture.
4. That a suitable incumbent has been in place for a minimum of a year so as to be able to appreciate the history and dynamics of the parish and church community.
5. That the parish can demonstrate an ability to function collaboratively in respect of its lay leaders, so that the shared exercise of ministry in the local church would be enlarged, not diminished, by the presence of a curate or trainee minister.

Appendix 4

Criteria for the appointment of Training Incumbents

It will be evident that the Training Incumbent has a pivotal role in the post-ordination phase, requiring particular gifts in practical theological reflection and the ability to supervise a minister in training. The Training Incumbent will be expected to work within the regional partnerships, to undertake training in supervision skills and to be willing to be under supervision. The requirements for being a Training Incumbent are set out in the following proforma which dioceses may wish to use either as a checklist when considering a person for the appointment or for the use of potential training incumbents in making the case for suitability for this role.

Training Incumbent proforma

1. Models strategic, reflective, theological thinking in parish leadership;
2. Engages regularly in in-service training and takes time for reading and reflection (Study week?);
3. Takes time for prayer and reflection (Daily Office, Retreats);
4. Is self-aware, secure but not defended, vulnerable but not fragile;
5. Has demonstrated a collaborative approach in discussion, planning and action in the parish;
6. Has been able to let go of responsibility to others, after appropriate training and supervision;
7. Has shared ministry, including difficulties and disappointments, with colleagues;
8. Has a personal theological and spiritual position which is creative and flexible so as to be able to engage and work constructively with different theological and spiritual positions;
9. Has a record of allowing colleagues to develop in ways different from their own;
10. Has an ability to interpret the social dynamics of the parish and to develop a strategy for mission and the implementation of change;
11. Has a genuine desire to be part of the training team rather than wanting an assistant and is therefore willing to agree to enable training experience that makes use of prior experience;
12. Has the ability to help the curate in the process of integrating his/her theological studies with ministerial experience.

Future expectations

1. Will undertake further study to function as a Training Incumbent;
2. Will give time to supervision and planning of training;
3. Is willing to receive supervision in the role of the Training Incumbent;
4. Will invest effort in mobilizing available resources, outside as well as within the parish for the training of a curate;
5. Will give the Initial Ministerial Education, IME, programme a high priority and work in partnership with diocese and Bishop's officers.

Appendix 5

Supervision

A successful supervising minister will be able to:

- Model lifelong learning and effective, reflective ministry which is mission-shaped;
- Give an account of a variety of pedagogical methods for skills-based learning and apply them to the context of curacy, suggesting incremental activities to meet the range of published learning outcomes;
- Identify and build relationships with others who share responsibility for the curate's learning, including lay people within the church, ecumenical and secular partners;
- Give a theological and experiential account of the importance of supervision in the life of the Church;
- Give a theological and experiential critique of a variety of models of oversight; accountability and supervision from within and beyond the Christian tradition;
- Structure an appropriate supervision relationship, e.g. through a learning covenant, with a training minister;
- Help the training minister to handle the supervision/oversight relationship (establish boundaries) within multi-layered community of relationships (the local ministry setting and other shared tasks);
- Work within competence level of the training minister;
- Support and challenge the training minister;
- Work with the obvious issues of ministry and development and the hidden dynamics of projection and power relationships;
- Make effective use of the supervision of their own supervising;
- Write evidence-based reports and discuss these with their training minister.

It is envisaged that training in supervision skills, in particular, might be delivered by an academic institution belonging to the local regional partnership. Several such courses are now running at M level, e.g. through Anglia Polytechnic University, delivered by the Cambridge Theological Federation. The syllabus covers such topics as:

- Theologies of oversight and supervision within the Christian churches;
- Accountability, discipline and discipleship;
- Appropriate models of supervision for a theological and ecclesial context;
- Appropriate use of insights from non-theological disciplines e.g. management theory regarding topics such as managing conflict, managing change, developing and sharing vision, and counselling regarding topics such as power, projection, transference and boundary;
- Skills of mediation, negotiation and reconciliation;
- Experience in being supervised and exercising a supervisory role;
- Critical theological reflection upon the practice of supervision.

The churches however, will need to retain responsibility for ensuring that all the learning outcomes for supervising ministers are delivered and for ensuring that supervising ministers are being appropriately supervised themselves. If training is delivered ecumenically there will be enrichment in terms of the dialogue and new thought possible, but particular attention will need to be given to the dynamics appropriate to the early years of ministry and lines of accountability and responsibility in each ecclesial tradition. It is recommended that if training is offered to ecumenically diverse groups, it is designed and delivered by an ecumenical team. It may also be helpful for others involved with the training minister's learning to take a course in supervision, for example, those involved in mentoring, trainers and those supervising training incumbents. Although theological institutions in a number of places are offering courses in pastoral supervision validated at M level there is no suggestion here that supervising ministers should have to have an M level qualification, merely that some of the skills of supervision are M level skills.

Appendix 6

The pattern of the trainee minister's working life and the minister's working week

The commonly inherited culture of the Church in which endemic patterns of chronic overwork and stress are a received expectation must be challenged by ensuring that the new IME has built into it the expectation of a much more spiritually, emotionally and physically healthy ministerial work-life balance. That is why the elements of the post-ordination phase of IME must be designed together as a coherent whole.

Nobody should wish to encourage a 'jobsworth' or 'clock-watching' mentality among the Church's ministers and some trends towards a 'fortress curacy' accessible only in 'office hours' must equally be resisted as incompatible with a ministerial vocation. Proper recognition needs to be given to the unevenly distributed pressures of the ministerial life. The principle must be observed that the proper relationship between the person of the minister and the role the minister takes in the church and community has its foundation in establishing a healthy balance in the different areas of the whole life of the minister as Christian disciple and as public servant of the gospel. There needs to be discussion towards a shared perspective between ministerial institutions and dioceses in endorsing a healthy ministerial lifestyle.

Commitment to engaging fully in the work of ministry and the 'Sabbath principle' both need to apply. Two recently developed 'rules of thumb' may be found helpful:

- The working week should be reckoned as 5.5 days with 1 full day off each week plus the evening of the day before that. As there is evidence that clergy commonly ignore the 'evening before' aspect of this, because of events in the local church, congregations need to be helped to respect the importance of time off for ministers.
- Strongly committed lay Christians commonly give up to 10 hours per week to church-related activities, and also commonly work around a 40-hour week in their employment. Since ministers are Christian disciples, so the logic goes, a reasonable maximum expectation of a minister's working week should be around 50 hours. This does not, of course, resolve the question of what counts as ministerial work.

At this point an important theological principle and an important practical reality need to be observed, which apply to all ministers, including trainees.

- The theological principle is that just as conversion to Christ and baptism in his name involve the giving of the whole of a person's life to the Lord and his service, so it is the whole person who receives ordination in response to the call of God that is recognized by his Church. It is in this sense that serving Christ as an ordained minister is far more than 'just a job that I do for God'.
- The practical reality is that the ministerial life involves actions, processes, roles and relationships that need to be given their proper weight, shape and coherence if they are to be carried through effectively in collaboration with fellow Christians and fellow ministers. This means that setting the proper boundaries of time and responsibility to ministerial activities and relationships is an essential part of surrendering the whole of life to the service of God as a baptized Christian and an ordained minister.

Ministerial boundaries recognize the integrity of persons, create limits to what can properly be expected, enable clarity of role and offer opportunities for space in which ministers and the people with whom they serve can grow in their God-given humanity, discipleship and witness.

Without this attention to appropriate boundaries in the ministerial life, there is the risk that the exercise of public ministry can become over-conditioned by those personal preferences of the minister that feed on the insatiable demands of congregations and communities that have become unwittingly trained in strong elements of demand and dependency.

All of this means that trainee ministers need to have proper written working agreements and training plans that take into account all of the elements of the IME to which they are to be committed, and that can form part of the basis of their work with training incumbents and other supervisors. Good quality, principled and realistic working agreements form a strong basis for ministerial freedom, direction and effectiveness. Among other things, they give permission to the trainee minister about what they need not necessarily do. They also enable other members of the church to understand more fully the balance that is needed between Christian discipleship and different aspects of Christian ministering.

Appendix 7

Membership

Parameters of the curriculum Task Group

Revd Canon Dr David Hewlett
(chair) Principal of Queen's Foundation, Birmingham, member of the Educational Validation Panel, Ministry Division

Dr Andrew Mein
Old Testament Studies Tutor, Westcott House, Cambridge, Member of the Educational Validation Panel, Ministry Division

Revd Canon Gordon Oliver
Director of Ministry and Training in Rochester diocese, Chair of Governors of SEITE training course; Chair of Ministry Development Officers' Network

Revd Dr Janet Tollington
URC representative; Director of Studies in Old Testament, Westminster College, Oxford

Revd Dr Roger Walton
Methodist representative: Director of the Wesley Study Centre, St John's College, Durham

Dr David Way
(secretary) Theological Education Secretary, Ministry Division

Post-ordination phase of IME Task Group

Revd Canon Roger Spiller
(chair) Director of Ministry and Diocesan Director of Ordinands in Coventry diocese; Chair of Ministry Division's Continuing Ministerial Education and Development Panel

Revd Lesley Bentley
Training incumbent and responsible for CME1–4 in the diocese of Ripon and Leeds

Revd Betsy Gray-King
URC representative; Education for Ministry Phase 2 office for the URC

Revd Dr Jane Leach	Methodist representative; Director of Pastoral Studies at Wesley House, Cambridge
Revd Canon Gordon Oliver	Director of Ministry and Training in Rochester diocese, Chair of Governors of SEITE training course; Chair of Ministry Development Officers' Network
Dr David Way	Theological Education Secretary, Ministry Division
Revd Jane Rawling	(secretary) National CME Officer Ministry Division